DIGITAL MARKETING STRATEGY

DIGITAL MARKETING STRATEGY

CREATE STRATEGY, PUT IT INTO PRACTICE, SELL MORE

NIKO LAHTINEN

Principal Owner and Commercial Director, Suomen Digimarkkinointi Oy, Finland

KIMMO PULKKA

Partner and Head of the Content Marketing Unit, Suomen Digimarkkinointi Oy, Finland

HEIKKI KARJALUOTO

Professor, Faculty of Information Technology, University of Jyväskylä, Finland

JOEL MERO

Assistant Professor of Marketing, School of Business and Economics, University of Jyväskylä, Finland

Cheltenham, UK • Northampton, MA, USA

Cover image: mymind on Unsplash.

Published by
Edward Elgar Publishing Limited
The Lypiatts
15 Lansdown Road
Cheltenham
Glos GL50 2JA
UK

Edward Elgar Publishing, Inc.
William Pratt House
9 Dewey Court
Northampton
Massachusetts 01060
USA

A catalogue record for this book
is available from the British Library

Library of Congress Control Number: 2023937048

This book is available electronically in the **Elgar**online
Business subject collection
http://dx.doi.org/10.4337/9781035311316

MIX
Paper from
responsible sources
FSC® C013056

ISBN 978 1 0353 1130 9 (cased)
ISBN 978 1 0353 1132 3 (paperback)
ISBN 978 1 0353 1131 6 (eBook)

Printed and bound in Great Britain by
TJ Books Limited, Padstow, Cornwall

CONTENTS

TO THE READER

Digital marketing is a critical part of a business because its success largely determines the success of sales. The success of the sales, in turn, determines the growth rate of the organization. Therefore, digital marketing jobs are some of the most sought-after jobs and its experts are some of the most sought-after employees. In addition, the COVID-19 pandemic has forced organizations to digitalize rapidly (from spring 2020 onwards), further increasing the need for digital marketing. Despite these factors, there are not many fresh books available on digital marketing—until now. You are currently holding one of the newest books in your hands, looking at it on your screen, or listening to it on your headphones. Great!

This book will teach you how to design a digital marketing strategy and measurably develop digital marketing and sales processes in key channels. The lessons of the book are applicable to the marketing of most companies but are especially well suited to those companies whose purchasing of their product and service offerings requires judgment and is not based on an impulsive "I'll buy the same again" or "I'll try that novelty this time" type of buying behavior. Because of this emphasis, the core message of our book is related to buyer personas. With buyer personas, you will learn to plan digital marketing better based on the behavior of potential and current customers. In this case, marketing is not an intrusive sales speech to customers, but a free and helpful service.

Our book consists of two parts (Figure 0.1). The first part deals with the strategic analysis and planning of digital marketing. The second part consists of the operational activities of digital marketing, which should be based on thorough strategy work. The second part also provides a practical description of how digital marketing is implemented in different channels and how the results obtained in them are measured. At its heart is the MRACE® (Measure, Reach, Act, Convert, Engage) model, which is based on the world's best-known digital marketing model, the RACE (Reach, Act, Convert, Engage) model, and serves as an excellent guideline from digital marketing design to operational implementation. At the end of the book, we open the door onto the work of a digital marketer and reflect on the direction in which digital marketing will be evolving in the coming years.

Our frame of reference, which we explore in detail in this book, consists of two phases: (1) strategic analysis and planning and (2) operational implementation. Together, they determine a company's ability to succeed in digital marketing. We mainly use the term *company* in the book, but the issue of the book is also applicable to other types of organizations. What makes the framework unique is that it combines strategic-level planning with practical action. Thus, it offers a more holistic view of digital marketing than that found in previous frameworks, which in our view focus either on the strategic level (leaving the reader responsible for planning practical concrete actions) or on the operational level (failing to provide the reader with the tools required to build a strategy for operational actions).

The first step in digital marketing is therefore strategic analysis and planning. The first step starts with an analysis of the company's business environment and the changes that take place in it. From the point of view of digital marketing, the most important variables of the business environment are naturally related to the digital environment, and the most important of these are changes in customer behavior and field of competition and, technological development. If

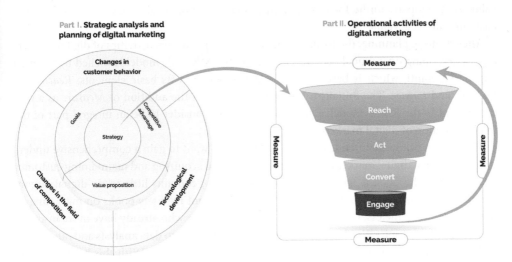

Figure 0.1   The structure of the book

a company does not understand how it will position itself for these changes in the operating environment, it will be impossible to plan for the future.

After analyzing the changes in the operating environment, the company can begin to design a digital marketing strategy. A *digital marketing strategy* refers to a company's long-term plan for how it will achieve its digital marketing goals in a changing business environment. The strategy consists of the following three areas: (1) setting goals, (2) determining the competitive advantage, and (3) the value proposition and value creation. The goals of digital marketing are largely determined by the role that digital marketing plays in the marketing and business as a whole. In any case, the objectives should be as specific as possible in order to guide the company's strategic and operational activities in a clear way.

Whatever the goals, achieving them requires that the company has a degree of competitive advantage. The definition of this advantage is crystallized in the question: How is the company able to meet customer needs in a way that competitors are unable to meet them? To answer this question, a company needs to gain an in-depth understanding of customer needs (by creating buyer personas) and the factors that set a company apart from its competitors (differentiation).

Once a company knows how it is able to meet customer needs in a way that sets it apart from its competitors, it should make a clear value proposition in a way that turns the company's competitive advantage to the customer's benefit. A good value proposition answers the question of what kind of value a company offers to a customer, which is why it is worthwhile for the customer to choose that particular company over its competitors. The promise of value is at the forefront of the communication of digital marketing, but without value creation strategies that support the fulfillment of the promise it is mere verbiage. The value proposition creates expectations for the customer, and the ability of value creation strategies to meet those expectations ultimately determines the customer experience. The customer experience, in turn, determines the success of digital marketing, that is, whether digital marketing generates value for a company in the form of new customers, additional sales, referrals, and a higher customer life cycle value.

After strategic planning, the focus can be set on the operational activities of digital marketing. In describing operational activities, we utilize the MRACE® model launched by Suomen Digimarkkinointi, which is based on the RACE model and its basic elements: *Reach, Act, Convert,* and *Engage.* The initialism MRACE® comes from the addition of *Measure* as a new component to the RACE model, a component that we consider to be an integral part of the implementation of digital marketing.

The book is primarily intended for those of you who want to gain a comprehensive understanding of what digital marketing is and how it relates to acquiring and maintaining customer relationships. The book is written to be reader-friendly, contains little to no digital jargon, and its message is easy to understand, even if you have not read any books on marketing or sales before. Nevertheless, the book is also suitable for those who already have more in-depth knowledge of this topic. We also warmly recommend the book to data analysts and others who look at digital phenomena more from the technology perspective. With this book, you will learn how to enable the operations of both a small and a giant organization to enter the era of digital sales. If companies are already making single trades worth more than €100 million completely online, what will be the situation in five years' time?

Do we need a book on digital marketing? Would a book on just marketing alone not be enough? In our view, traditional strategic marketing books work well in supporting strategic analysis and the planning of digital marketing. However, as a whole, traditional marketing books deal with marketing very broadly and do not highlight the specific features of the digital environment in strategy formulation. An even clearer shortcoming relates to the tactical implementation of digital marketing, which is covered very little in most marketing books. Although marketing and business have digitized at a rapid pace and we can think of dropping the *digital* from *digital marketing* as it will be implied, it is not yet time for that. *Digital marketing* is talked about; it is being conducted and taught as *digital marketing* for the time being. That is why our book also talks about *digital marketing* and not just *marketing.*[1]

Enjoy reading this book!

Niko, Kimmo, Heikki, and Joel

NOTE

1.   The text has been through a double-blind review process.

GLOSSARY

DIGITAL MARKETING TERMINOLOGY

A/B testing	A user research method that compares two different options and selects the one that works best for them. Typically, users are shown two different versions of a website or ad. A/B testing is done a lot in different areas of digital marketing, ranging from Google search engine advertising to Facebook advertising and improving newsletter content.
Algorithm	A set of rules or process that describes how a task is performed. In digital marketing, for example, an algorithm determines what content is displayed to users of the services. Examples of content generated by algorithms include ad serving and newsfeeds in Facebook and Google search results.
Bounce rate	The percentage of users who leave immediately, for example, users leaving a website.
Buyer persona	The type of customer that a company wants to get or a person that describes the target group.
Competitive advantage	How an organization manages to meet customer needs in a way that competitors are unable to meet.
Conversion	Achieving a defined goal, such as downloading a guide, subscribing to a newsletter, or making a purchase.
Conversion rate optimization (CRO)	Optimizing the conversion to achieve a defined goal, such as getting users or website visitors to act in a desired way. In digital marketing, it most often means improving the saleability and ease of use of a website through the information gathered through various tools.
CPA	CPA stands for *cost per action*. In digital marketing, CPA refers to a bidding model in which the advertiser only pays for a certain conversion, that is, for a specific action to be completed. For example, CPA is used in advertising, and the advertiser only pays for the specified results.
CPC	CPC stands for *cost per click*. In digital marketing, CPC refers to a bidding model in which an advertiser pays for clicks.

CPM

CPM comes from the words *cost per mille*. CPM tells you what it costs to reach a thousand people. Also known as CPT (cost per thousand). CPM refers to ad impressions and is a way to bid where you pay per views.

CTR

CTR comes from the words *click-through rate*. It tells you how many readers of a particular piece of content—such as a newsletter, an advertising campaign, or content on a website—click on a particular link.

Digital marketing

All marketing that utilizes digital technologies. A more precise definition is: Developing and communicating a value proposition in digital media to selected buyer personas based on strategic analysis.

Digital marketing strategy

An organization's long-term plan for how it will achieve its digital marketing goals in a changing business environment.
The strategy comprises three areas:
1. setting goals
2. the determination of competitive advantage
3. the value promise and value creation.

Display advertising

The visual advertising or marketing communications on a website. Display advertising includes text-based ads, images, moving image (video), and audio. The term is currently used for all banner advertising.

Driver

The factor that most influences the purchasing decision of buyer personas. Most commonly, it refers to the value that a product or service produces, the problem it solves, or the need it fulfills.

Google Ads

Google's online advertising program, which manages advertising on Google. It includes search engine advertising, advertising on the Google Display network, and YouTube video advertising.

Google Analytics

Google's analytics service, used for tracking website traffic.

Hotjar

User tracking software that visually displays what the user has done on the website. It is most commonly known for heat maps and recorded website visits.

Impression

The number of times an ad or search result was displayed.

Influencer marketing

Collaboration with people who have influence over other people's behavior, such as their buying decisions. In addition to celebrities, influencers are bloggers and tubers who directly or indirectly promote their products and services to their followers, especially through social media channels.

Key Performance Indicator (KPI)

KPI refers to the most important indicator with which to measure performance. The term KPI is commonly used in business. In digital marketing, it typically measures things related to the sales process, such as the number of leads, the number of users from a particular source, or purchases from an online store.

Keyword

A word that a user types into a search engine or an internal search on a website when searching for information about something. The term *search term* is also used.

Landing page

In digital marketing, a *landing page* is a single web page that a user is directed to by clicking on a link from elsewhere on the web (such as a link in a search engine, newsletter, or advertisement). The landing page is typically sales driven, directing the user to a specific action (e.g., ordering).

Lead

A potential customer—either a person or a company—who has already shown some interest in the company, for example, by leaving his or her contact details with the company.
In marketing, a distinction is often made between a *marketing lead* and a *sales lead* depending on how far the potential customer is into the buying process and whether the lead is processed by the company's marketing or sales.

Marketing

Acquiring new customers and engaging current customers.

Marketing automation

Software and technologies that are used to automate and streamline marketing. For example, marketing automation software sends a thank you message to a user's email inbox after the user has made an online purchase or downloaded a guide.

MRACE® model	An operative tool for digital marketing. The initialism MRACE comes from the words: *Measure* *Reach* *Act* *Convert* *Engage* The MRACE model was developed by Suomen Digimarkkinointi.
Native advertising	A form of paid advertising in which the content being advertised adapts to and is consistent with other content in the publication. Native advertising can therefore be difficult to identify as advertising. For example, an online text about sleep problems may include native advertising by bed stores.
Organic traffic	Visitors coming to a website for free, for example, from search engines.
Programmatic buying	Buying advertising with an advertising tool from around the web, from various ad networks and ad auctions.
Remarketing	Marketing to a user who has already visited a website that happens outside of the website (e.g., in an ad network, via email, or via social media).
Search engine	A software system that systematically searches the Internet (typically websites) for information.
Search engine advertising (SEA)	Text and image advertising on search engines (such as Google) where an ad is displayed in a user's search results based on the user's keyword, location, and the budget set by the advertiser.
Search engine marketing (SEM)	The marketing done in a search engine. Search engine marketing includes search engine optimization (SEO) and search engine advertising (SEA).
Search engine optimization (SEO)	Improving the organic visibility of a website in search engines.
Top-of-mind marketing	Marketing that is used to keep the brand in the minds of potential or current customers.
Website traffic	All the visitors coming to the website.

PART I
STRATEGIC ANALYSIS AND PLANNING

1
An introduction to digital marketing

Digital marketing has become a widely used term since the 2010s, most typically referring to marketing that utilizes the most important digital platforms of our time. These platforms include websites, email, search engines, social media, and mobile applications. In practice, the term digital marketing does not differ significantly from other, previously used terms—such as *Internet marketing, online marketing,* or *e-marketing*—and broadly means the same thing: all marketing using an electronic device or the Internet.

Thus, digital marketing can be broadly defined as marketing that utilizes digital technologies. It is difficult to provide a more precise, generally accepted definition of digital marketing. The concept is ultimately determined by what digital technologies an organization adopts for its marketing and by what the organization means by the term *marketing*. This, in turn, is primarily affected by the role given to marketing in the company. Marketing responsibilities may include (1) making or supporting sales, (2) customer communications and/or brand building, (3) customer relationship management, (4) gaining customer understanding and implementing it in the organization, (5) creating value for customers, or (6) any mix of these responsibilities.

The strategic level of marketing also varies across organizations. Marketing can be understood as (a) a set of marketing activities, (b) an activity of an organization with certain resources, or (c) the voice of the customer in the company, where every employee in the organization is collectively responsible for gaining customer understanding and utilizing it in business development.

Due to different conceptualizations of marketing, different individuals and organizations can refer to very different things with the terms marketing and digital marketing, which can lead to misunderstandings. To avoid this, it is paramount to say what digital marketing means in each case. In this book, digital marketing means developing and communicating a value proposition (based on strategy analysis) to selected buyer personas via digital media. It aims to acquire new customers and engage existing ones.

Our definition of digital marketing above sums up the following three priorities of this book:

1. Our book underscores that digital marketing is not just the operational design and implementation of communications in order to drive sales—the core of communications is based on market analysis, competitive advantage, and the value proposition built on the analysis.
2. The book focuses on digital marketing communications, such as search engine marketing, social media marketing, and website design. (We will review these in more detail in the second part of the book.)

3. Our book emphasizes the sales revenue approach, where, as a result of marketing communications, a company increases sales by acquiring new customers or increasing the life cycle value of its existing customers.

Digital marketing is also defined more comprehensively than developing and communicating a value proposition (based on strategy analysis) to selected buyer personas via digital media. For example, the American Marketing Association, the scientific umbrella organization for marketing, has defined digital marketing from a more organization-oriented perspective, defining it as activities, institutions, and processes that leverage digital technologies to communicate and create value for customers and other stakeholders. Similarly, digital marketing researchers Kannan and Li (2017) defined digital marketing as an adaptive and technology-assisted process by which companies collaborate with customers and partners to create, communicate, share, and maintain value for all stakeholders. The overall strength and weakness of these scientific definitions is roundness, which improves generalizability but impairs comprehensibility; after reading such definitions, few of us really understand what the definitions really mean. Therefore, we recommend using our own, relatively simple definition.

1.1 DIGITAL MARKETING HISTORY AND ITS CURRENT STATE

The starting point for the technological development of marketing is difficult to determine, but probably, the first major digital technology involved in marketing was the computer in the 1940s. This was followed by, among other things, barcodes in the 1950s, and bank and credit cards in the 1970s (which set out to collect digital data on customer transactions and goods flows for the first time). By far the most important technology related to digital marketing has been the Internet, which was born in the late 1960s. However, its widespread use only began after the World Wide Web and the first graphical web browsers were developed in the late 1980s and early 1990s.

We next divide digital marketing and digital business into three different waves to make it easier to understand their development. The history of digital marketing and digital business is built in these waves (Figure 1.1).

1.1.1 The first wave of digital marketing

Marketing on computers and mobile phones began to gain a foothold around the mid-1990s. Soon, courses on e-business were offered at universities, addressing this rather significant revolution. The emergence of graphic Internet browsers in the early 1990s ushered in the first wave of what is today known as digital marketing. That is when many of the digital services we still know first saw the light of day. These include banks' websites and their affiliated online banks, search engines (like Yahoo, Altavista, and Google), and the first online stores (like Amazon and eBay). This new way of doing business was then referred to as *electronic business*. Correspondingly, the term *electronic marketing* was used for matters related to the sale and marketing of these services.

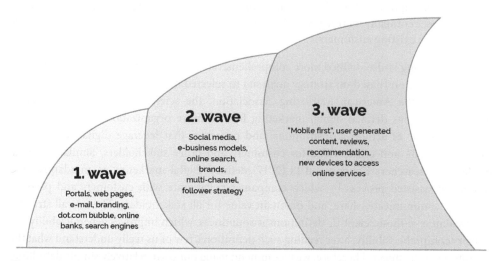

Figure 1.1   The history of digital marketing and business

The challenges of the first wave of digital marketing were particularly related to the uncertainties of electronic business (or *e-business*): *electronic commerce* (or *e-commerce*). For example, data derived from e-commerce revealed that nearly 70 percent of products were rejected at the shopping cart stage due to uncertainties such as payment, delivery, and purchase risks. This first wave, on the other hand, has also been seen as the golden age of digital marketing. This was the time when the first websites were constructed, and e-commerce was launched. The means of online marketing were mainly banner advertising, the websites themselves, and the slowly emerging field of email advertising.

Early entrants were initially successful: they sold a lot and gained market share. However, due to the large number of entrants, the situation began to change rapidly, and many players were disappointed with the small revenue streams and the negative operating profit. Indeed, in the early years of the millennium, the world's first Internet bubble emerged as the market began to better understand what digital business and marketing were all about and how huge expectations resulted in successful or unsuccessful businesses. After the dot.com bubble burst, only strong players and brands survived. It has been said that 30 percent of the disappointments during the first wave was due to the global recession in technology markets and 70 percent was due to the disappointments of online business itself.

Marketing returned to more traditional multi-channel thinking and multi-channel marketing, where it was understood that buying would continue to take place in traditional brick-and-mortar stores as well. It was realized that not all purchases would go online. At the beginning of the millennium, for example, Levi's completely stopped online sales because it caused distribution channel conflicts (i.e., problems between stores and e-commerce) and was inefficient. In the late 1990s, there was also a strong belief that clothes could not be sold online because customers wanted to try them on. This estimate was later proved completely wrong as clothing is one of the most purchased online products in the world.

1.1.2   The second wave of digital marketing

The second wave of digital marketing is considered to begin with the emergence of social media services in the mid-2000s even though these platforms were hardly thought of from a business or marketing perspective during this wave. At that time and shortly thereafter, the world's most used social media platforms were developed, such as LinkedIn (2003), Facebook (2004), YouTube (2005), Twitter (2006), and Instagram (2010).

However, the number of users of these social media rulers did not grow as fast in the beginning as they do on today's fastest growing channels. For example, TikTok grew by nearly 400 million users between 2019 and 2020. It took Facebook four years to reach the 100 million user limit, but in just about two years (2010–12) it increased its user base from 500 million to one billion. In Finland, for example, Facebook only started to become more widespread a few years after its establishment, in 2008–09.

The second wave is described as an era of more advanced business models, online searching, brands, multi-channels, and follower strategies. It is worth remembering that although the current giants of social media were born at this time, they had almost no commercial content in these early days. Facebook, for example, was a network service with no advertising and no content of any kind produced by organizations. Therefore, during the second wave, these channels were hardly thought of from a business or marketing perspective and served other purposes, mainly communication between people.

One thing that also contributed to the closure of Nokia's mobile phone business happened during the second wave. The first iPhone came onto the market in 2007, completely revolutionizing the use of online services and giving birth to numerous new players in the industry. The iPhone was the first phone with easy-to-download apps and a touch screen that worked properly. With smartphones, the Internet came with us everywhere, forever. This development laid the foundation for the third wave of digital marketing in which we are now living.

1.1.3   The third wave of digital marketing

The third wave of digital marketing began around 2015 and is centered on the transition of the Internet to mobile devices. The key drivers of change are generally considered to be content marketing, the transformation of social media platforms into advertising platforms, and "mobile first" thinking (where websites and e-shops are primarily designed for smartphones). The explosive growth of online content and online users has contributed significantly to the emergence of the third wave.

User-generated content (UGC)—such as blogs, videos, product reviews, discussions, and testimonials—has further enhanced the social nature of the Internet. This has led organizations to want more control over the publication of UGC in an effort to influence audiences and get positive reviews. Many companies began to take the first steps towards utilizing UGC in marketing. Over the years, this phenomenon gave rise to various commercial collaborations and influencer marketing.

In terms of devices, in addition to the smartphone, the third wave has brought to our homes the tablet, the smart TV (Internet-connected TV), and a number of other devices that allow us to access, for example, YouTube content. As smartphones have not changed very significantly since 2007, we are eagerly waiting for one of the smartphone manufacturers to come up with the next real breakthrough model that includes something completely new. It will create the conditions for new mobile services.

The third wave has also brought to our consciousness new terms such as *artificial intelligence* (AI), *augmented reality* (AR), and *location services*. In many contexts, what these terms mean in practice has remained completely unknown for the end users. Most of the things related to AI and augmented-reality applications are behind the services we already use. Thus, AI, AR, and the applications we use are slowly being integrated; for example, Facebook uses AI to select the ads that are displayed to each of us and mobile services use location information to collect our location data on an ongoing basis.

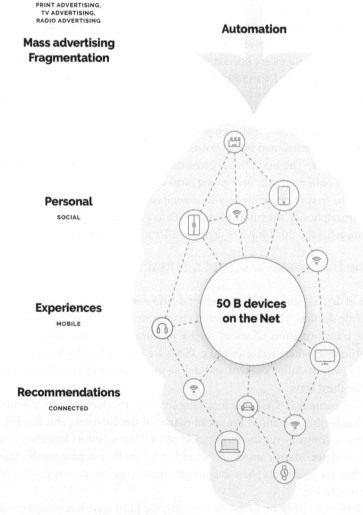

Figure 1.2   Understanding digitalization

From fragmented mass advertising—which includes print advertising, TV advertising, and radio advertising—we are entering an era of personalization, experiences, and recommendations (Figure 1.2). This era is further illustrated by the increase of automation and the connection of 50 billion devices to the Internet (e.g., our refrigerators, telephones, and industrial devices). Digitalization and automation are present everywhere in our environment.

BOX 1.1 THE EFFECTS OF THE COVID-19 PANDEMIC ON DIGITAL MARKETING

The global coronavirus pandemic has affected the marketing field in many ways. However, it has had no effect on the main message of this book as the theories, frameworks, and models we present have not lost their function due to the pandemic. Rather, the pandemic has strengthened them as it has forced every organization to take the much-talked-about digital leap. The whole world is now moving at a rapid pace towards digital sales.

From a digital marketing perspective, the pandemic has had an impact on the use of digital services, which has increased in all respects since March 2020. The number of website visitors has increased and e-commerce has grown across industries—in some industries exponentially, especially in the home electronics and hardware. Toys, leisure equipment, and products related to learning have also been sold significantly more than before. Indeed, according to McKinsey (2020), the pandemic accelerated online shopping by ten years in just 90 days. People's shift to remote work has increased the sales of home-related products. In Finland, for example, the K Group's online food store sales grew by 800 percent in the first six months of the pandemic and home electronics retailer Verkkokauppa.com's stock price rose by 70 percent between spring 2020 to the end of the same year. On the other hand, victims have been, for example, luxury goods, tourism, and the sales of new cars.

More generally, from a business perspective, the pandemic has affected companies in many ways, and it remains to be seen how the sectors most affected, such as tourism and aviation, will recover from the pandemic. In this pandemic, companies are divided into two camps. The first camp consists of those whose products have more buyers than they can in some cases sell to, such as those selling food, household goods, electronics, pet food and supplies, and medicines and vitamins. The trade-in of used cars also exploded in the summer of 2020, when people switched from public transport to private cars for fear of coronavirus. The second camp is made up of companies whose demand for products and services is constrained due to the pandemic, such as tourism and restaurant companies, airlines, and event organizers.

The pandemic has also had a significant impact on marketing budgets, including digital. In the UK, for example, advertising fell by almost 50 percent in the spring of 2020. Advertising budgets clearly reflect the above-mentioned effects of the pandemic on various industries. McDonald's advertising fell 97 percent while Microsoft increased its advertising by 142 percent. In Finland, the total amount of advertising decreased by 28 percent in June 2020, and in October, there was a further decrease of 7 percent compared with the previous year. The amount of advertising in Finland has even followed demand during the pandemic: media advertising has been boosted by advertisers in telecommunications services, pharmaceuticals, and the financial sector whose products are being more actively purchased during the pandemic. In terms of advertising, online advertising's return to a growth trajectory in Finland after the collapse of summer 2020 was noteworthy; at the end of the same year, it had already grown by 4 percent. Advertising grew the most on social media and search engines. Search advertising accounts for about half of the euros spent on online advertising, while social media advertising is the second largest form of online advertising, accounting for about 40 percent of online advertising in Finland.

1.2   MARKETING MODELS AS PART OF DIGITAL MARKETING

Now that we have created a brief overview of the history and current state of digital marketing, we turn our attention to something more permanent: marketing models. They form a very central part of our book, which is why we will briefly explain them at this stage.

Many may wonder why we need to use marketing models. Do they not restrict activity? Yes, marketing models limit activity, but that is only a good thing. In marketing and business in general, it is as important to know what things can be left out as it is to know what to invest in. Models provide a tool for understanding a particular phenomenon.

With the help of models, marketers and decision makers can structure their work more clearly and always speak the same language. The models tell you how many different channels an organization should be in and which channels will help the organization achieve its marketing goals. The models guide you to the correct marketing as performance declines and guide you to pain points that, after being fixed, will lead to the greatest profit improvements.

The situation sometimes faced in marketing can be compared to the following situation faced by a car repairman: If a car repairman is presented with a car and is told, "The car is broken," most of his or her time goes into troubleshooting. The same situation arises in the context of marketing, for example, when a sales manager finds that there are not enough leads (i.e., potential buyers). There is only a very circular problem that is impossible to solve immediately without looking at the whole marketing process. However, if the problem is highlighted using a model, it immediately leads to a solution, for example: The traffic to a company's website is clearly high quality because the content on the site is read for a long time and shared a lot. The number of website visitors has also increased. However, there are too few leads, so the company should focus first on how to turn the readers of the content on their site into leads.

Similarly, an organization may set a marketing goal of increasing the number of invitations to tender in a six-month period from one invitation to tender per week to five invitations per week. While the goal is precise, it is very difficult to start creating a marketing strategy without dismantling the current state with the help of a model. You can get more requests for quotes, for example, by getting more traffic to your pages from Google search results, search ads, banner ads, social media, or through affiliates. On the other hand, the number of requests for quotations from the existing traffic can be increased by improving the usability and content of the site. The utilization of existing customers and their recommendatory power must also be taken into account. So, there are many options, and with limited resources it is not possible to implement all of them.

For example, when you use a model to resolve an issue and take into account data from a website visitor-tracking program, such as Google Analytics, your organization may notice that most of the requests for quotes come from Google's paid advertising for certain keywords. Based on this information, it can close the worst-performing ads with confidence and use the free budget to advertise using the keywords that perform well. In this way, the models crystallize the problem directly into solutions. They tell you the steps you need to take to get your customers' interest and guide them from the first encounter to becoming your committed customers. The models also make it easier to get the kind of customers that every organization craves: satisfied, engaged, committed, and high-buying customers who act as referrers to the company.

There are certainly hundreds of different marketing models, but in this book, we will focus on the MRACE® model, which we think is the most useful digital marketing model of all. We will cover the model in more detail in Chapter 4 of this book. However, at this point, let us take a brief look at the general marketing models on which most of today's most-used digital marketing models are based.

1.2.1 Generic marketing models

Digital marketing models are based on traditional marketing models. We first introduce two so-called marketing process models (Figures 1.3 and 1.4). They help you deepen your understanding of what marketing and sales are all about in the end. Digitalization has not changed the basic theoretical assumptions of marketing science, such as those involved in these process models that describe marketing.

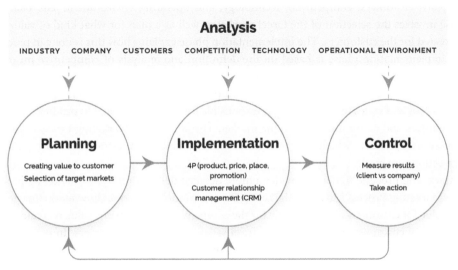

Figure 1.3   Marketing Process Model 1

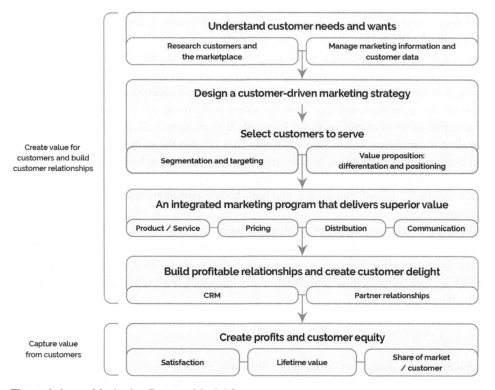

Figure 1.4   Marketing Process Model 2

Of the marketing process models, Marketing Process Model 1 is the basis of all marketing. According to this model, marketing is managed through analysis, planning, implementation, and control. The model states that the analysis phase includes an analysis of the industry, company, customers, competition, technology, and operating environment. The planning phase involves the selection of the target market as well as a plan for what kind of value will be created for the customers. The implementation phase explains how this is done in practice. The implementation phase is based on the definition and analysis of competitive means of marketing, the so-called 4P model (that derives its name from the four words *product*, *price*, *place*, and *promotion*), and customer relationship management. The 4P model was developed in the 1960s and states that marketing is responsible for decisions related to products, pricing, distribution, and communication to the market. The last step of Marketing Process Model 1 is the control phase, in which the achieved results are evaluated in relation to the set goals and then actions are made.

Marketing Process Model 2 provides a more detailed description of the marketing process than Marketing Process Model 1. Marketing Process Model 2 describes how marketing generates value for customers and ultimately for the company. For a company, value is created from the value of customer processes, that is, from satisfied and loyal customers. In other words, a company's customer base is at the core of a company's value creation process. Creating value for customers always starts with understanding the customer's needs and wants. It includes customer and market research and the management of customer data and market information. This knowledge is used to develop a customer-centric marketing strategy and to select target markets. This value creation process involves segmentation (i.e., dividing a company's customer base into different parts according to certain selected criteria and serving selected segments), as well as decisions related to value proposition, differentiation, and positioning (i.e., how the company positions itself from a market perspective, such as image). Next, value creation must develop an attractive offer for selected customer segments, that is, 4P decisions are made. It is then decided how customers can be engaged and how profitable customer relationships can be developed. At this stage, the customer relationship management strategy is decided. Finally, the value created for the customer is changed in order to develop the business. In marketing thinking, the success of value creation is measured by market share growth, operating profit, the growth of the overall customer base value, customer satisfaction, the customer life cycle value, and the share of wallet (i.e., how much a customer concentrates their purchases on a particular product category in a particular organization).

Digital marketing models are also based on these assumptions as marketing on digital channels is in no way different from basic marketing. The starting points are the same regardless of the channel or medium used for sales and marketing. Thus, the traditional marketing process models work as well as universally valid theoretical models for digital marketing. Still, a few more specific frameworks have also been created for digital marketing. These include the digital marketing model of Kannan and Li (2017; see Figure 1.5) and the model presented in *Marketing 4.0*, written by Kotler, Kartajaya, and Setiawan (2017; see Figure 1.6).

Kannan and Li's model is based on the marketing process models mentioned above in which marketing is seen as a function and activity that creates value for customers and translates customer value into value for the company. According to the model, digital technologies (such as devices and marketing technologies) affect all three marketing processes, that is, they affect customer buying behavior, a company's marketing decisions (such as 4P decisions), and value generation. Kannan and Li's model can be interpreted as relating a significant change in the marketing process to a change in customer behavior, the effects of which are reflected in a company's marketing decisions and value generation. In terms of changed customer behavior, they highlight, for example, the growth of search engines, social media, and UGC. These factors increasingly determine how customers search for information and make choices.

In the model presented in *Marketing 4.0*, digital marketing is placed with traditional marketing at the conceptual level. According to the model, traditional marketing thinking—such as the thinking upon which segmentation, brand differentiation, the 4P model, and value creation are based—is not disappearing and creates the basis for digital marketing thinking. Digital marketing is thus built on top of traditional marketing, being an add-on to it. In the model, digital marketing plays a more important role than traditional marketing in generating so-called hard outcomes, such as sales, because digital marketing is more measurable. The MRACE® model presented later in this book is based on this very idea of more measurable marketing.

In the model presented in *Marketing 4.0*, traditional marketing involves segmentation, brand differentiation, 4P decisions and sales, and value creation. Traditional marketing is important (especially in the early stages of the buying process) for generating awareness and

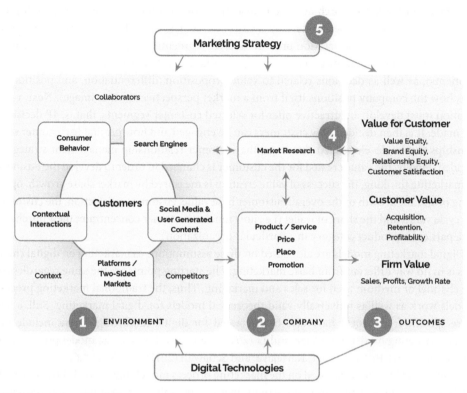

Figure 1.5 The digital marketing framework of Kannan and Li (2017)

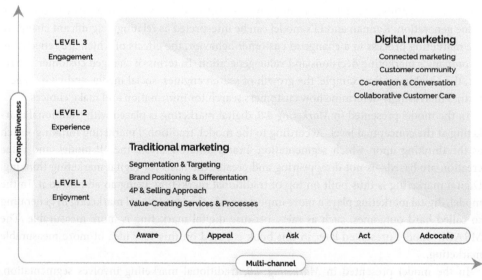

Figure 1.6 The digital marketing model of Kotler et al. (2017)

interest. In this model, digital marketing includes a connected marketing approach, customer communities, value co-production and discussions, and collaborative customer service. According to the model, the importance of digital marketing increases as we move from the inquiry, purchase, and recommendation stages of the purchasing process (we discuss the purchasing process in more detail in Section 2.3). The combination of traditional marketing and digital marketing thus provides the greatest benefits in terms of competitiveness and market share.

2
Analysis of the digitalized business environment

Now that we have gone through the marketing models and processes, it is essential to understand into what kind of business environment the models are being integrated. The analysis of the digitalized business environment is an important part of the digital marketing strategy. The analysis ensures that the digital marketing strategy is linked to changes in the business environment that are relevant to the company's strategy. In this case, digital marketing will not become a separate tactical function but an integral part of the company's business.

In this chapter, we focus on three factors that have a significant impact on the digitalization of the market environment and thus on the design and implementation of digital marketing. These factors include changes in technology, the competitive landscape, and customer behavior.

The fourth important factor is formed of regulatory changes, such as the General Data Protection Regulation (GDPR) in the European Union (EU) and changing policies regarding using cookies. In the coming years, these will have a major impact on how digital marketing can be measured, targeted, and implemented in general. However, we will not go into these changes in more detail as the rate of change is such that there will have been so many changes in regulation since the time of writing that the information will have become outdated. Instead, up-to-date information on the EU's GDPR and data security can be found, for example, on the website of the Data Protection Commission.

2.1   TECHNOLOGICAL DEVELOPMENT

The development of technology is inextricably linked to digital marketing, and digital marketing is often defined as the use of technology in marketing. Marketing-related technologies can be roughly divided into front-end and back-end technologies. The front-end technologies are customer-interface technologies that are perceptible and available to the customer. Back-end technologies, in turn, refer to the technologies used in the internal processes of organizations. These technologies have an impact on the customer interface but are usually not directly perceivable by the customer.

2.1.1   Front-end marketing technologies

Front-end marketing technologies are technologies that ordinary users can detect and utilize. From the perspective of technological development, the most revolutionary front-end technologies have been web browsers, online stores, search engines, mobile devices, and social media. Web browsers revolutionized the usability of the Internet and allowed people to access the global information network. Online shopping revolutionized commerce and increased its internationality. Search engines revolutionized the ability to find relevant information and content on the Internet. Mobile devices, in turn, allowed access to the Internet regardless of location. Social media increased the speed of information sharing and, at least to some extent, democratized communication. Before social media, it was very difficult for the average person to create and share content or opinions with the general public because media houses acted as gatekeepers to published content. In the age of social media, anyone can publish content and the community decides which publication deserves attention. There are, of course, pros and cons to this, as many have certainly noted.

In the current technology environment, there are at least two new types of customer-interface technologies related to marketing that have the potential to significantly change the business environment. For the time being, however, their impact is limited to individual applications. The first of these types of technology is formed of virtual reality (VR) and AR. "Many people know of AR from AR games like Pokemon Go, which is why the impact of this type of technology is often most strongly associated with the entertainment industry. More broadly, the idea of merging physical and digital reality is radical and may, in the longer term, make the interfaces between the digital and physical worlds fuzzier. The importance of physical presence is diminished when you can sit in the comfort of your room in the physical world and simultaneously be in a virtual world watching a real-time sporting event from the best seats in the arena. The Facebook corporation, for example, renamed itself Meta after sharing its vision of building a huge "metaverse" over the next 10 to 15 years, which refers to a next-generation Internet based on VR that would blur the interfaces between the physical and digital worlds. In practice, users of the metaverse could "hang out" in the virtual world and encounter other people there in the same way as in the physical world. VR and AR can also facilitate the distance selling of complex offerings in business-to-business (B2B) markets. For example, it is difficult to drag a paper machine to a customer meeting, but the customer can visit the virtual world to learn about its physical details and how it would fit into their mill.

Another significant type of front-end technology that is in its early stages of development is related to virtual or digital assistants. Most of us know these as Siri, Alexa, and the Google Assistant. In practice, these digital assistants are so far mainly voice-based interfaces for searching for information or performing simple digital actions, and their use does not yet have very significant implications. However, as the applications evolve, their use will increase significantly. Many of us may still be alienated from voice-based interfaces because chatting with a computer or a bot feels weird. It must be borne in mind that listening and speaking are the basis of human communication and thus much deeper in our inheritance than writing and reading. When we encounter people in the physical world, we are more likely to exchange greetings by speaking than by writing. As digital barriers are removed, it is logical to think that the interfaces of the future will be increasingly based on speech rather than on writing.

Why does this have business significance? Because, as digital assistants evolve, we can search for information and make purchasing decisions without the need for a computer screen. "Siri, what does *digital marketing* mean?", "Alexa, which running shoes should I buy?", "Google, order me food for a week." We will increasingly be able to perform such tasks in the future with the help of digital assistants, which will reduce the need to stare at different screens. The idea behind such a scenario is that personal digital assistants will get to know us thoroughly, so their ability to complete tasks and make purchasing decisions based on our personal needs and preferences will perhaps even grow to a proactive level. An assistant would procure products for us that we might not realize we needed.

The scenario sounds futuristic, and many may even consider it dystopic. In terms of research, however, it is fascinating in many ways. A digital assistant that would base product recommendations on objective facts would, at least in theory, most likely lead to better purchasing decisions and make brands virtually irrelevant. If the assistant were to dig up all the information we needed from the depths of the Internet, what would happen to advertising? Would the moment finally come when advertising—or at least advertising that the consumer does not want—comes to an end? Hardly. As the old saying goes, "marketers ruin everything" in the end by turning an authentic utility service into a commercial platform. This is what happened to search engines and social media, so there is no reason to believe that this would not be the case for digital assistants as well. In addition, it should be remembered that all the leading players in the industry represent the world's largest commercial technology companies. Indeed, this raises questions about data ownership, consumer espionage, and privacy protection—the concerns these questions address have led to a significant slowdown in the adoption and diffusion of digital assistants.

2.1.2   Back-end marketing technologies

Back-end technologies are technologies that are not directly perceptible to consumers. These technologies enable the background processes needed to measure, target, and personalize digital marketing, for example. Most back-end technologies are related in one way or another to data processing and management. The most significant back-end marketing technologies include customer relationship management (CRM) systems, digital analytics tools, marketing automation, and the Internet of things (IoT).

The widespread adoption of CRM since the 1990s has contributed to a shift in marketing philosophy—it has shifted from transactional trading to gaining and growing profitable customers. The emergence of digital analytics at the turn of the 2010s made it possible to track digital footprints. It provided new ways to gather data about customers' digital behavior, such as customers' navigation paths on a company's website, the keywords used in search engines, or the opinions expressed on social media. Web analytics (e.g., Google Analytics) and social media monitoring software (e.g., Brandwatch) are examples of digital analytics tools that can be used for collecting data on customer behavior.

Towards the end of the 2010s, marketing automation established itself as one of the most widely used marketing tools. It enables companies to automate routine tasks and decision-making situations, but also to target, personalize, and schedule marketing communications activities according to predetermined criteria. The IoT, in turn, has expanded the range of devices from which data can be collected into the company's systems. Importantly, while most marketing technologies have traditionally collected data on customer encounters at the pre-purchase and purchase phases, IoT allows data to be collected on post-purchase product use. In the past, product usage data may have been collected from digital services, but the IoT has made this same opportunity available to physical product manufacturers.

In recent years, the main drivers of the development of back-end technologies have been the growth of (1) big data, (2) AI, and (3) the computing power of computers. By *big data* we mean large and diverse masses of data that contain, in addition to numbers, unstructured data types, such as texts, images, videos, or voices. In practice, *unstructured data* refers to the types of datasets that are difficult to organize into a spreadsheet or formula. About 80 percent of the data collected by organizations is unstructured,[1] and as this data has been very difficult to analyze, organizations have generally made decisions based on structured or numerical data.

AI and its subcategories, such as machine learning and deep learning, have developed significantly in recent years and enabled the analysis of unstructured data, such as image recognition, audio-to-text translations, and text-based theme recognition. The exponential increase in the computing power of computers, in turn, has made it possible for big data to be processed in the first place. Without going into the technical details, an illustrative example of increasing computer power is that a modern smartphone has more computing power than the combined computing power of all the NASA computers of the 1960s. Yet people were sent to the moon using those NASA computers.[2]

In terms of digital marketing, the growth in big data, AI, and computing power means we can collect and analyze increasingly diverse data on customer behavior and market movements in order to support decision-making. If the data used in digital marketing in the past was largely based on customer clicks, likes, conversions, and sales figures, we will be better able to interpret social media conversations and content related to customers or other stakeholders, as well as identify new customer needs and problems from customer dialogues such as chatbot discussions and customer service phone calls. These are significant opportunities and these may change the marketing orientation so that it becomes more strategic, shifting the focus from operational cost efficiency to identifying new growth opportunities and improving the customer experience.

2.1.3 The selection and adoption of technologies

Digitalization has brought new technologies to marketing at an accelerating pace, which can offer companies new opportunities to develop their competitiveness. However, in addition to opportunities, they also bring new challenges to companies and force them to innovate in order to remain competitive. The challenges are manifold, but the most important ones relate to the selection and adoption of technologies.

Since 2011, the Chiefmartec blog[3] has conducted an annual survey of marketing-related technologies. In the 2011 survey, it identified a total of 150 marketing technologies and stated that it is challenging for the organizations to be able to select the most appropriate of these for their purposes. Year after year, the number of technologies has grown rapidly, and in the 2020 survey, it identified a total of about 8,000 marketing technologies. These technologies are divided into six subgroups, presented here in order of magnitude: (1) social media and relationship management, (2) content marketing and customer experience, (3) e-commerce and sales, (4) data and analytics, (5) advertising and promotion, and (6) management and processes.

The number of marketing technologies has thus been multiplied by 50 in ten years. The result may be partly explained by more advanced methods being used for detecting technologies over the years. The fact is, however, that the number of marketing technologies has grown exponentially over the past decade. While most of the technologies listed may not be ground-breaking, the increase in numbers means that the technology landscape is becoming increasingly fragmented, and there are more and more providers of different tools. Consequently, it is becoming increasingly difficult for companies to conceive the big picture and choose the technologies that meet their business needs.

The question, "Which technologies or tools should we choose for digital marketing?" is one of the most common questions we encounter when meeting managers. As shown by the diversity of the marketing technology landscape described above, this question is difficult to answer without deep knowledge of the company in question. This is also, in most cases, the wrong opening question when considering suitable technologies for digital marketing.

When there are many different technologies to choose from, the focus should be on the organizational goals and problems that the company is trying to solve with the new technologies. It is also common that the solution to the problem is not a new technology but, for example, a change in the organizational routines and processes. In fact, technology itself is rarely the solution to any business problem, but rather, it is a tool that allows a company to operate more efficiently or produce better quality. Thus, technology enables the change of some activity. For example, there is a myth that the adoption of marketing automation would somehow miraculously automate the whole marketing process and immediately improve its effectiveness. In fact, marketing automation does not in itself automate anything, but the rules built into it and the processes built around it can enable more efficient operations, such as more personalized communication with current and potential customers.

In addition to the selection of technologies, their adoption has been found to be difficult. Technological developments are increasingly offering new opportunities, but the ability of organizations to adapt to the opportunities offered by new technologies has developed slowly. In most cases, a technology is worthless if its adoption does not lead to a change in routines. However, changing routines is notoriously difficult for people, and the integration of new technologies into organizational workflows is typically a very slow process, especially in large organizations. It is said that technology changes exponentially, organizations change logarithmically. Thus, the larger the organization grows, the slower the adoption of technologies in organizational routines becomes. This is one of the main reasons why digital-born start-ups are able to challenge dominant market players. They do not bear the burden of old routines, practices, and a massive information system infrastructure; they are able to adopt new technologies and practices in a more agile manner. Large companies usually have a resource advantage, while small companies have a speed advantage. A speed advantage is often crucial when talking about a rapidly changing technology environment.

Traditionally, the process of adopting technology in an organization has been initiated by first finding out the requirements and desires for new technology in the various departments or functions of the organization. The different options are then carefully assessed and a detailed plan for implementation is made. Only then is a purchase decision made, after which the actual adoption of the technology as part of the organization's operations can begin. Such an adoption process that emphasizes careful planning has been described as representing a *waterfall model*. The metaphor comes from the fact that the process proceeds systematically in one direction through defined steps, which eventually leads to adoption. The weakness of the waterfall model is that the process takes a long time—often years—before the appropriate technology is even selected. When the technology is finally adopted, it may well have been replaced by better solutions. For this reason, large companies have also started to implement more agile adoption processes as they have found that their traditional technology adoption processes are no longer suited to a rapidly changing digital environment. Thus, if in the past the adoption of a particular technology was considered, planned, and speculated about for years, now the decision may be made very quickly. The focus has shifted from careful planning to experimentation and continuous iteration.

The shift in focus in technology adoption processes is also due to the fact that many new technologies today represent cloud and software-as-a-service (SaaS) solutions. The cost of acquiring SaaS solutions is usually low, and many vendors also offer free trials or demo versions that allow for agile testing of the technology before making a purchase decision. Indeed, the adoption of technology is increasingly following a so-called agile model. Unlike the waterfall model, the agile model is based on iterative and flexible testing and learning. In the agile model, the technology can be tested in the planning phase before major investments are made. In the pilot phase, firms can explore and test the features offered by the technology, analyze the results, and learn from them. If the results are satisfactory, new use cases are gradually added and the user base expanded. Notably, the technology can be rejected at any time if it appears that it does not serve the needs of the organization.

The agile model of adoption also has its own pitfalls as it easily leads to technology-driven thinking. In that case, the choice of the technology to be tested may be based on the hype around the technology rather than on the actual business goal or problem. Another weakness is that technologies that appear useful but to which the organization cannot afford to commit resources may be chosen for the testing phase. As said before, technology is not the solution but the enabler of the solution. At the heart of the solution are the changes in routines and processes that are empowered by the technology. If an organization does not have the resources to build the new processes, there is no point in adopting even the most promising technologies. A technological orientation thus easily leads to the loss of the big picture. In the end, a firm may notice that it owns a number of relevant technologies with expensive licenses but does not make effective use of any of them.

In summary, today's marketing technology environment requires faster adoption processes and bold experimentation. It is paramount to start with the problems and needs of the business strategy in order to select the big changes in which the organization wants to be involved. There are countless marketing technologies, but it is not possible to test them all. Nor can an organization be involved in all technological changes at the same time. Instead, the focus must be on those that bring the organization closer to its strategic goals. This is where marketing models help a lot: they divide marketing activities into clear stages, and when the stages are measured with the right metrics, the figures reveal concrete problems at different stages. A well-defined problem cuts off a huge number of possible technologies, not to mention a huge amount of thought work.

In addition, the existing technological infrastructure and resources of the organization must be taken into account. It is important that it is possible to build interfaces between new technology and existing technologies so that the new technology does not become a silo and can be integrated into existing systems so that data moves from one system to another. A large proportion of companies also underestimate the resource needs required to adopt new technology. If an organization does not have sufficient resources, it should find the new technology so necessary that it will commit to acquiring the missing resources. As a result of these considerations, an organization is able to significantly narrow down the range of technologies that it sets out to experiment with using an agile model in order to adapt to the evolving technological landscape.

2.2   CHANGES IN THE COMPETITIVE LANDSCAPE

While digitalization and technological developments have shaped customer behavior, they have also led to significant changes in the competitive landscape. The term *hypercompetition* is increasingly being used to describe the competitive field globalized by digitalization, where competition is extremely fierce and sustainable competitive advantages are becoming increasingly difficult to achieve.

As early as the 1970s, Michael Porter developed the so-called five forces model (Figure 2.1) that provides a managerial tool for understanding the forces that shape industry competition and, on the other hand, help adapt strategy to the competitive environment. The five forces of the model are (1) rivalry among existing competitors, (2) the threat of substitute products or services, (3) the threat of new entrants, (4) the bargaining power of suppliers, and (5) the bargaining power of buyers. The first force of the model, "rivalry among existing competitors," describes the prevailing competitive situation in the industry, which in turn is constantly being shaped by the four other forces. Although the model is old, it is more relevant than ever and provides a meaningful framework with which to look at the changes brought about by digitalization in the competitive landscape.

Digitalization has increased *rivalry among existing competitors* in many industries for the simple reason that it has blurred geographical boundaries. The competition is no longer limited to local players and has become truly international. In the context of physical goods, longer delivery times and additional logistics costs could theoretically hinder cross-border

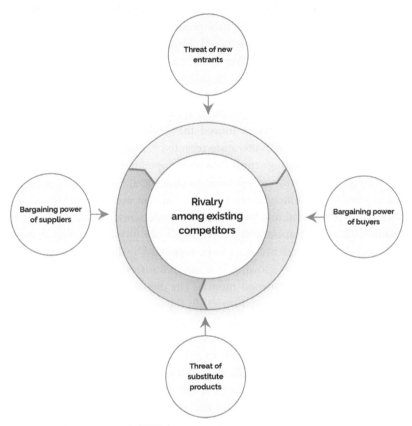

Source: Adapted from Porter (1979).[4]

Figure 2.1   The five forces that shape industrial competition

trade, but practice has shown otherwise. Many local traders are facing great challenges in responding to fierce international competition over prices and delivery times. Cloud services provide extreme examples of international competition because the purchasing process, product delivery, and usage are often fully completed via digital means. When we decide to acquire a new cloud service (e.g., Dropbox), from a technical point of view, it does not matter where the provider operates the service as long as the service works as promised. Of course, language skills can still be a barrier to buying if the service is not provided in a language the consumer understands.

Digitalization has increased *the threat of substitute products and services* in the competitive landscape. Technological developments are accelerating innovation cycles and new products are entering the market at an accelerating pace. What is particularly noteworthy, however, is that the product may no longer be replaced by a new and better physical product but may be replaced by a digital product or service. These digital products and services have disrupted many industries. A famous example of a digitizable product is digital cameras, which replaced analog cameras in a relatively short time after they were launched. Indeed, Kodak is often used as a warning example: it missed out on the development of digital cameras, with the result that its extremely strong international market position turned into bankruptcy in 2012. Similarly, well-known examples of replacing a physical product with a digital service include Spotify and Netflix, which have significantly disrupted the music and TV entertainment businesses. When was the last time you bought a CD or DVD? More and more consumers already lack the hardware to play them.

However, it is important to note that the threat of substitute products is also present in B2B industries. For example, the products of industrial companies are increasingly augmented by digital elements and additional services. Indeed, the servitization of industrial companies has gained a lot of attention in the B2B literature recently. Among other things, more and more industrial companies are collecting sensor data on the operations of their devices and building data-driven services that provide added value to customers. For example, such sensor data can be used to provide recommendations for more efficient use of the device or to anticipate maintenance needs, which lead to a better customer experience. In other words, even industrial companies no longer compete with the excellence of a physical product alone—they also compete with a customer experience that can be supported by digital and smart services.

The threat of new entrants is growing in many industries as digitalization has provided opportunities for new types of business models. The digital platform economy in particular has affected the dynamics of many industries. In the hotel business, AirBnB has developed a digital trading platform that allows individuals to provide accommodation to those seeking it and thus compete with traditional hotels. According to statistics,[5] the AirBnB platform had 7.7 million accommodation options globally in 2019, facilitating almost 430 million overnight stays during the year. It is clear that AirBnB will not replace the role of traditional hotels, but it will certainly affect their customer acquisition and pricing power. Uber has created a similar new entrant threat in the taxi business, and FinTech companies have done the same in the finance industry. Start-ups based on digital business models in general are constantly emerging to defy traditional players and their operating logics. Regulation often slows—but does not prevent—agile start-ups when entering the market.

It is more modern to look at the growth of *the bargaining power of buyers* and *the bargaining power of suppliers* as a whole and to talk about the changes in the power relations of the value chain that digitalization has made possible. For product manufacturers, digitalization has provided an opportunity to reduce the number and role of intermediaries in the value chain. Any company that makes products can set up an online store and start selling their products directly to end users instead of selling the products through wholesalers and retailers. Such direct sales to end users are called the direct-to-consumer (D2C) strategy. A successful example of such a strategy is the Dollar Shave Club, which grew into a billion-dollar company by selling one-dollar razors online that are delivered right to your door. Excellent digital marketing communications also played a key role in the Dollar Shave Club's success story, examples of which can be seen on YouTube.

However, succeeding in a D2C strategy is not easy as it requires a significant investment in reaching customers, earning attention, and building a brand. Many of us want to shop in online stores where competing brands and options can be compared. For this reason, in most cases, digitalization has increased the bargaining power of online marketplaces with a large and loyal customer base. An extreme example is Amazon, whose strong market position in the digital age has decreased the bargaining power of many product manufacturers. With Amazon's market share of over 50 percent in the US, many manufacturers find it unrealistic to opt out of the platform. Another example is DoorDash, which connects restaurants and customers with a mobile app. The greater the proportion of customers who prefer DoorDash as a digital marketplace for restaurants, the weaker the bargaining power of restaurants in relation to DoorDash. The strong bargaining power of food delivery platforms is probably one of the main reasons for their high market valuations.[6]

2.3   CHANGES IN CUSTOMER BEHAVIOR AND TRENDS

Digitization offers consumers and customers an unlimited variety of media, content, and other offerings. Together, they offer new opportunities for information retrieval, enjoyment, taking care of affairs, socializing, and so on. These opportunities have shifted customer behavior in the digital direction. Although most use of digital channels is not related to purchasing or other commercial matters, digitalization has still had a significant impact on customers' purchasing decision-making processes and customer behavior.

Understanding changes in customer behavior is one of the most important research topics in marketing science. Some of the authors of this book are also part of a research team that has been working for about 20 years on understanding the changes in buying behavior and the growing role of digital tools and services in it. During this period, the importance of traditional

Figure 2.2   A buyer in the digital era

marketing has steadily diminished in the world of the digital consumer. Recent textbooks on marketing have shifted the focus of marketing from traditional marketing to digital interaction with the consumer.

In this section, we focus in particular on changes in the customer's purchasing processes. To better understand digital age customers, it is worth looking at how shoppers today use digital tools and services. In the buying processes of buyers in all age groups, they increasingly rely on search engines, information on corporate websites, a brand's website, price comparison sites, booking sites, reviews and comments from other users, online discussions, social media content, and influencers (Figure 2.2).

2.3.1   The buying process

The traditional idea of the customer purchasing process dates back to the 1960s and is based on a five-step model. The five steps follow: (1) awareness, (2) an information search, (3) evaluation of the alternatives, (4) the purchase decision, and (5) post-purchase behavior (Figure 2.3). The model starts with the idea that the customer becomes aware of a need, either by perceiving a problem or by getting some external stimulus (e.g., by seeing an advertisement that makes him or her aware of the new buying need). The customer will then start looking for information on potential offers and comparing different options until he or she ends up making a purchase decision. Finally, the customer uses the product or service, evaluates the success of the purchase decision, and possibly makes a positive or negative recommendation to others.

Figure 2.3   The customer buying process

The model has persisted in the marketing literature and has lasted exceptionally well over time. Although numerous variations have been proposed for the model, its basic idea has not changed significantly. It is often argued that digitalization has revolutionized the buying process. This is true, but looking at the big picture, it is hard to argue that the steps presented in the model would still not be included in much of our purchasing decisions. Perhaps the buying process is not always quite as straightforward as the model suggests, and we move back and forth between evaluating alternatives and searching for information. Sometimes we may make very impulsive or routine purchases, in which case we do not actively search for information and actively compare alternatives. However, in purchasing decisions that require consideration, the model still accurately describes the decision-making stages that the customer goes through in her or his purchasing process.

Thus, digitalization has not so much revolutionized the logic of the purchasing process but has rather affected the manifestation of the various stages of the purchasing process and the activities associated with them. For example, digital advertising, content marketing, and social media discussions have brought new stimuli to the customer with which she or he becomes aware of her or his needs. Digital channels offer new ways to search for information and compare alternatives. The purchase can be made digitally from an online store, in addition to which, the customer has a better opportunity to share his or her experience of the product or service that he or she purchased through a product review or social media post. In this way, the customer can also influence other people's purchasing decisions.

To understand the digital consumer and his or her buying behavior, we also need to understand how purchasing decisions are structured: what facilitates buying, what factors slow down buying, and what factors act as barriers to making a purchase. According to the book *Marketing 4.0* (Kotler et al., 2017), rational purchasing takes place through the following five stages: the awakening of awareness, appeal, ask, act (purchase), and ultimately onto recommendation. Most of the change in the buying process takes place in the buyer's network. Therefore, organizations need to think about how they can get into the buyer's network through marketing. At least we can say that the solution is not product-centric pushing—it must purely be thought of from a customer perspective. What content does an organization need to provide on different channels at different stages of the buying process? What content arouses buyer interest? How do you get a buyer to recommend a product or service she or he buys? Does the buyer act rationally or do habits, emotions, and routines guide buying?

In order to identify potential buyers, it is necessary to know the different purchasing decision paths and buyer personas. At what stages of the buying process do customers experience the biggest problems? How do you get a customer to move from one step to the next? How do you get the customer to interact with the brand at different stages of the purchase? To help answer the questions, you can use, for example, a funnel model that describes the different types of digital content that are usually used at different stages of the purchasing process.

2.3.2   Research findings concerning customers in the digital era

According to research, consumers make extensive use of information available on the Internet when making purchasing decisions. For example, 95 percent of car buyers use the Internet to buy a car.[7] The car is selected online, and the role of the car dealer is to act as the physical supplier of the car. Most buyers have already made their decisions when they step onto the dealer's premises. In addition, kitchen buyers behave in the same way: 90 percent of kitchen renovation buyers have been found to make use of online content, especially during the consideration phase of their purchasing process.[8] For larger purchases, about 80 percent of consumers search the Internet for information before making a purchase decision.[9] Digital content plays a huge role in today's buying process, even if the purchase itself is made through a physical channel.

Together with the market research company Taloustutkimus, we have been collecting data on the purchasing behavior of Finnish consumers over a period of three years, including collecting data on how much consumers use various sources of information when buying. More than 6,000 consumers have participated in the surveys, and the samples represent Finns by gender, age, and place of residence.

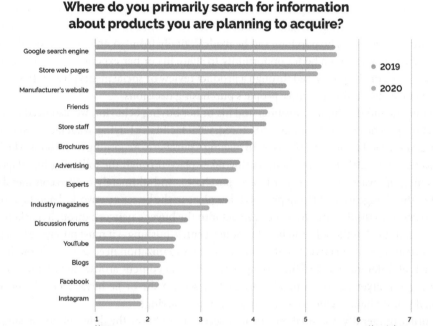

Figure 2.4   The information sources used when Finnish consumers make purchases

According to adult Finns, the three most important channels in their search for information are the Google search engine, a store's website, and the manufacturer's website (Figure 2.4). In contrast, social media held very little importance as an information retrieval channel. Has social media been overemphasized in recent digital marketing if its importance as an information retrieval channel is minimal based on other surveys too? The answer is not unequivocal as consumers using social media are currently being heavily exposed to advertising and other commercial content, the effects of which cannot be fully captured in these kinds of surveys. The effects are thus both subconscious and such that they may not be remembered or reported in such surveys. Few of us read a blog to look for information about a product, but reading a blog can actually give rise to an entire purchase intent.

HubSpot conducted an interesting consumer survey in 2017 by asking consumers where they search for information about a brand they like. According to the survey, the brand's website is by far the most visited source of information (visited by 67 percent of the respondents). Just under half of the respondents (41 percent of them) watched videos of the brand and 37 percent liked the brand on Facebook. In contrast, only 16 percent of the people started following the brand on Instagram, 14 percent followed the brand on Twitter, and 6 percent followed the brand on Snapchat. Only 15 percent of them read a blog, 12 percent joined a forum, and 12 percent posted about the brand on social media. Only 8 percent of the respondents did not search for information about the brand at all (Figure 2.5).

If you like a certain brand, how do you search for information about it?

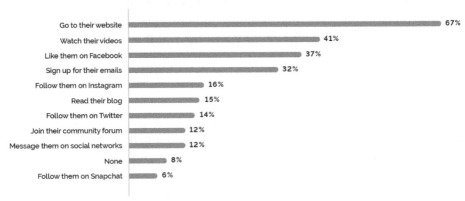

Source: Modified from HubSpot (2017).[10]

Figure 2.5   Where do consumers search for information about a brand they like?

We collect here some fresh facts about digital consumers:

- 90 percent of Finns aged 15–25 use their mobile phone for searching for additional information while visiting a store[11]
- 84 percent of US consumers aged 18–29 use their mobile phone to shop online
- 87 percent of US consumers aged 18–60 start their shopping journeys from either Amazon or Google
- 77 percent of US consumers aged 18–60 search for information in store using their mobile phone, while only 35 percent preferred to ask a shop assistant for help[12]
- 50 percent of Finns over the age of 65 often or almost always search for information on Google when purchasing products or services.[8]

2.3.3   Business buyers' behavior

The purchasing behavior of organizations has been studied much less than that of consumers. The studies conducted still convey one main message about the behavior of business buyers: The buying behavior of business buyers has been converging with the buying behavior of the digital age consumer all the time. The business buyers' purchasing process has been outlined as consisting of the following six steps: identifying the need, defining product features, conducting research, making a selection, making a purchase, and conducting an evaluation. However, the nature of the product or service being purchased has a significant impact on how we understand the purchasing behavior of business buyers. It is a different matter to buy office paper or hand sanitizer for a company than it is to buy a nuclear power plant or 60 fighter jets. The role of digitalization in companies' purchasing decisions must always be understood in terms of the nature of the solution that is to be purchased. Although we are not very well informed about the purchase processes of nuclear power plants or fighter jets, digital content is also expected to play a significant role in them.

Accenture conducted an extensive survey for business decision makers in 2017. According to the study, business buyers go through more than half of their buying process before they have any contact with the seller. More than half (61 percent) of B2B sales transactions start online. One interesting consequence of the digital age is that, according to this study, 90 percent of business customers do not answer a sales call from someone they do not know (e.g., from an unknown number). This result reinforces the idea that organizations need to enter the customer's buying process through their marketing by creating engaging content, not by trying to force themselves into the buying process.

Accenture's survey interviewed 1,350 sales and customer service executives from B2B organizations around the world. In the survey, 71 percent of B2B business leaders said that their business customers increasingly want a similar service experience to what they get as a consumer in a non-business context. Interestingly, half of the executives interviewed admitted that they were unable to provide such a customer experience for their clients.

Toman, Adamson, and Gomez (2017) have investigated what slows down a B2B customer at different stages of the purchasing process (Figure 2.6). According to the participants in the study, in the early stages of purchasing, the problem is to retrieve useful information. There is too much information and it is difficult to find useful information. Sound familiar? People become a problem in the middle of the buying process: when sellers get involved in a customer's buying process, problems often arise. In the final stage, the problem is having too many options. The majority (86 percent) of sellers consider it important to offer all possible options to the customer. However, the more options there are, the harder it is to make a choice, which slows down the entire purchasing process. In addition, the excessive number of options causes nearly half (40 percent) of B2B buyers to experience post-purchase uncertainty (cognitive dissonance).

Like the Accenture study, Toman et al. (2017) found that more than half of B2B buyers spend a lot of time in the buying process before making first contact with a seller. In the survey by Toman et al., 65 percent of B2B customers say they spent as much time on the initial stages of the purchasing process (i.e., on searching for and comparing products or services) as they expected to spend on the entire purchasing process. So, we should make purchasing easier as few business buyers have idle time.

According to a recent survey,[13] B2B buyers consider reviews (64 percent), product demos (43 percent), and videos (33 percent) to be the top three forms of digital content they use in the buying process. Just over half (61 percent) of B2B shoppers thought that relevant content was the main driver for a certain behavior (such as a purchase or an invitation to tender). The survey involved 500 B2B buyers and sellers from the US.

These studies are important for those marketers who want to reach B2B customers because the studies provide a foundation for designing a content strategy. If you are a B2B business decision maker, consider whether you offer content on your website or other digital channels that is relevant to the information seeker or buyer and whether that content is easy to find. Has

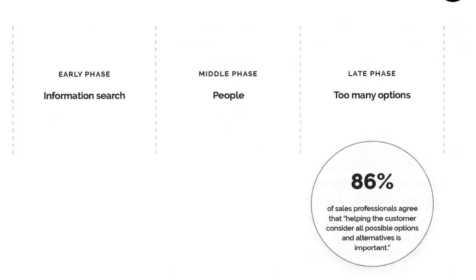

Figure 2.6   Barriers to making a purchase among B2B buyers

information retrieval been made easy? Do you offer too many options online? Is buying from your business made easy? Or is it as cumbersome as making an e-invoice? Actually, the easiest thing to think about is: Does the content on your company's website serve your customers as well as your best customer service representative and your best seller? If not, then your company's website has huge development potential with which the company can snatch more market share if it realizes this potential.

We will take a closer look at making buying easier, building a website, and the content of a website in the second part of the book.

2.3.4   Consumers' information overload

Increased information—especially on social media and in email and online content—has created a whole new kind of problem and field of research. In the fields of information technology, education, and psychology, the effects of the increased flood of online content on people's behavior and brains have been studied in recent years.

Psychological research shows that social media has several side effects on people's mental health. People who are on the verge of depression or who are already suffering from depression are particularly vulnerable to these effects. The huge flood of information on social media and in online content has led to the so-called fragmented attention phenomenon, where a person's attention is drawn to too many things at the same time and his or her ability to concentrate is impaired. Fragmented attention negatively affects many of our practical matters, such as our work. Nothing happens if we try to do too many things at once.

Often, consuming digital content can be a waste of time. Sometimes you find that you spent hours searching for information about a product using website content and finding the cheapest place to buy the product when you could have bought it from a local market for one euro more than the price on Amazon. On the other hand, for example, we spend less time buying a home, which is one of the biggest purchases of our lives, than we do on planning a kitchen renovation (which studies show usually takes more than a year).

LEGO also provides a good example of the limited capacity of the human mind to handle a large number of options. LEGO has a product called Creator that allows you to build several different models from the same LEGO blocks. The Creator package can now be made into three different models, which has made the product family very popular. Previously, the Creator package was sold as a package with 12 models, but consumers did not buy it. LEGO has justified the simplification of the Creator package by saying that the 12 options were not understandable to consumers, so LEGO simplified the number of options to three. According to the CEO of LEGO at the time, their starting point is to keep things simple and easy to learn.

The human brain contains 20 megabytes of RAM, which is no more than four typical digital images. Our brains are only able to process a very small amount of information at a time, and we are not as intelligent as we often think we are. With age, the ability to process information deteriorates significantly, especially with regard to creative thinking. According to a study by NASA, by the age of 25 we have retained only about 5 percent of the creative thinking we had when we were five years old.

So, the human mind is often lazy and we do not always act rationally. Take this into account and make buying as easy as possible on your website.

2.3.5   Customer empowerment

Digitizing customer behavior has significantly changed the power relations between companies and customers for the benefit of the customer. If we think about the customers' buying process before the Internet, the consumer's options were narrower and the seller almost always had more information about the products and services than the customers. If you needed a new jacket, for example, you probably drove to the city center, where there were a few relevant clothing stores from which to choose. There were a few jackets in the stores that suited your needs, and the sellers provided more information and recommended certain products. So, you relied heavily on your experience and the seller's recommendations, unless you happened to be a particularly dedicated jacket expert. In other words, sellers had clear information power over customers.

Today, the power relationship has turned in the customer's favor, and the phenomenon is called *customer empowerment*. The increased customer empowerment can be divided into four sources of power:[14] demand-, information-, network-, and crowd-based power (Figure 2.7).

Demand-based power suggests that, in the digital world, consumers have access to a vast variety of alternative products and services. Thanks to digital channels, products and services can now be purchased globally from a variety of players instead of from a few local players. In the digital world, every competitor is, so to speak, one click away, increasing the range of products and services available. From a business perspective, this means that competition has become tougher and more international, highlighting the importance of genuine competitive advantages.

Information-based power, in turn, suggests that digital channels make it easy to access product and service information in a variety of content formats that help customers make

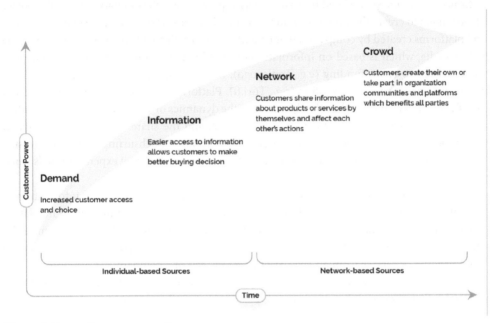

Figure 2.7   Four sources of consumer power

better purchasing decisions. For businesses, this means they need to produce content on themes that customers are looking for information on and that will help them make good purchasing decisions. At times, companies fear that sharing free information will also give competing companies information that will benefit them or that it will help customers buy from competitors as their understanding grows. While this fear may be partially justified, companies should be more concerned that competitors will provide better content to customers, making it difficult for the companies to get involved in the customer buying process. When a company creates content and provides it for free to its target audience, it creates a routine in which their customers visit their website. At the same time, it builds an image of the company's expertise.

Network-based power suggests that customers can also create their own (user-generated) content and share their experiences and opinions about companies and their products. They can also participate in the sharing and discussion of the content produced by companies and write product reviews. By doing so, consumers have more power to influence other people's purchasing decisions. Network power can have a significant (positive or negative) impact on a company's success. Bad products and services are harder to market, and so, the customer experience and fair treatment of customers play a big role. Negative experiences often spread like wildfire, while a good customer experience often leads to positive testimonials and recommendations. One of the most interesting consequences of network-based power is that the company's most profitable customer may not be the one who spends the most money on the company's products and services, and may be the company's advocate or an influencer who has influence over other people's decisions.

Crowd-based power is related to network-based power and refers in particular to the power of customers to create their own communities and platforms or to participate in communities and platforms created by companies that benefit all parties. Probably the best-known example is Wikipedia, which is based on information created by users. Other examples include platforms related to crowdfunding (e.g., Indiegogo), the sharing economy (e.g., Couchsurfing), and consumer-to-consumer trading (e.g., Tori.fi). Platforms based on collective power often benefit consumers and, on the other hand, affect the dynamics of some industries: Tori.fi offers a virtual flea market that increases product lifetime, and the share of trading second-hand goods increases at the expense of the share of new goods. Couchsurfing allows you to stay overnight at the houses of the community members instead of booking expensive hotels when traveling.

To sum up, digitalization has provided customers with more options and information at their disposal than ever before, which significantly increases their bargaining power in relation to companies. Customers also have a better opportunity to influence the decisions made by other customers and, in some cases, the opportunity to ignore companies, allowing them to buy a product or service from an ordinary person instead of a company. As a counterbalance to customer empowerment, companies, in turn, have more data on customer behavior at their disposal, which increases the companies' opportunities to influence customer behavior.

NOTES

1. Forbes (2019).
2. ZME Science (2021).
3. https://chiefmartec.com/.
4. Porter (1979).
5. Alltherooms (2021).
6. DoorDash acquired Wolt (valuation €7 billion) in November 2021.
7. Google & ComScore (2017).
8. Sawhney (2011).
9. GE Capital Retail Bank (2013).
10. HubSpot (2017), HubSpot Content Trends Survey Q3.
11. Karjaluoto (2021).
12. Salsify (2017).
13. Uberflip (2021).
14. Labrecque et al. (2013).

3
Digital marketing strategy

A *digital marketing strategy* refers to a company's long-term plan for how it will achieve its digital marketing goals in a changing business environment. It is sometimes said that a company's long-term strategic plans are no longer meaningful because the digitalizing world is changing so fast that strategies become obsolete before they are implemented in the organization's operations. Many believe that in a digitalizing world, it would be wiser to just make bold experiments and agile changes based on the data generated by the experiments.

We agree that the world is changing rapidly, and that is why it is critical to continuously analyze the changes in the digital business environment that we described in Chapter 2 in order to build a foundation for a digital marketing strategy. It is also very important to make bold experiments and data-driven decisions, but these should be in line with the strategy. Otherwise, marketing activities appear perplexing in the eyes of the customer, resulting in a confusing customer experience and brand image. The strategy therefore provides clear guidelines and boundaries for digital marketing, within which even quick experiments and decisions can be made. While the details of a strategy can quickly become obsolete today, differentiating yourself from competitors in a way that creates customer value remains the most essential part of any marketing strategy.

Goals are the starting point for a digital marketing strategy. In Section 3.1, we present the different goals of digital marketing and explain how to make them as concrete as possible. Once goals are set, the digital marketing strategy culminates in a plan for how the goals will be achieved. In practice, achieving the objectives requires a competitive advantage, which generally refers to the characteristics of the firm that enable it to beat its competitors. From a marketing perspective, competitive advantage means that a company is able to satisfy customer needs in a way that competitors cannot match. Building such a competitive advantage requires an in-depth understanding of customer needs as well as the ability to differentiate the firm from competitors. In Section 3.2, we discuss the two cornerstones of building a competitive advantage: *creating buyer personas* (see Section 3.2.1) corresponds to gaining an in-depth understanding of customer needs, while *differentiation* (see Section 3.2.2) corresponds to a firm's ability to differentiate itself from its competitors.

Once a company has defined its competitive advantage—that is, once it has an in-depth knowledge of customer needs and knows how to differentiate itself from its competitors—it must turn that competitive advantage into a value proposition. A good value proposition is based on the company's competitive advantage, and its idea is to concretely communicate the value that the customer receives when purchasing the company's products or services. In other words, it briefly answers the question of why a customer should do business with a given company from among all the options. However, a value proposition is just a set of empty words unless the company is also able to deliver on its promise (i.e., to create the value that it promises to the customer). For this reason, in Section 3.3, we present value creation strategies that allow a company to deliver on its value proposition.

3.1   SETTING DIGITAL MARKETING GOALS

The goals of digital marketing provide the basis for strategy work. The goals must be relevant to the business, and their main task is to clarify the strategic outcomes that the company wants to achieve with its digital marketing. These goals cannot be too many in order for them to have strategic weight. In setting goals, the main emphasis is on making strategic choices and setting priorities. For example, if you set sales growth as the first strategic goal for digital marketing, it is often unrealistic to set reducing marketing costs as the second goal, because increasing sales usually requires financial investments that increase costs.

In turn, focusing on just one goal can lead to a narrow-minded approach in digital marketing. For example, simply having the goal of increasing sales may guide marketers to focus on promotional campaigns that typically have a positive sales impact but a negative impact on profitability and brand value.

As a rule of thumb, we recommend setting three to five goals for digital marketing so that the goals have strategic weight but do not focus too narrowly on one area of improvement, such as increasing sales. If there are more goals, you should try to prioritize them or divide them into a few main goals and related subgoals, which can make them easier to manage. However, it is important to note that goals should guide strategic choices—making a long list of goals is just as ineffective as not setting goals at all.

Because digital marketing goals are based on a company's business strategy and are therefore company specific, it is difficult to take a position on what the good or bad goals are in digital marketing. However, in the following, we will review the main types of digital marketing goals (the 5S—*sell, serve, speak, save, and sizzle*—goals) and the criteria that can be used to make the goals as concrete as possible (the SMART—specific, measurable, assignable, realistic, and time-related—criteria).

3.1.1   The 5S goals of digital marketing

The 5S goals[1] provide a concrete way to divide digital marketing goals into five different categories. The 5Ss that give the typology its name are the different goal categories: *sell, serve, speak, save,* and *sizzle*. We will introduce the goal categories in more detail below.

Sell is perhaps the clearest and easiest to understand goal of digital marketing—digital marketing must generate sales in both the short and long term. As we will see later in the book when discussing the MRACE® model, most of the practical implementation of digital marketing is related to the goal of increasing sales.

However, increasing sales may mean slightly different things in different industries and contexts. When it comes to e-commerce for consumers, digital marketing is often aimed at direct sales. In other words, a company performs actions that bring buying customers to the company's e-commerce store. In the case of the B2B industry, where final purchasing decisions are often made in sales negotiations, digital marketing is more about supporting sales and influencing the customer's buying process. Sales are also supported by the presentation of customer recommendations or references in digital channels. In customer references, the customer typically describes his or her customer experience and the benefits he or she has received from the firm's product or service. Another concrete action is to digitize sales support materials, such as product demos, videos, and animations.

In practice, supporting sales through digital marketing often refers to sales lead generation. *Sales leads* are potential customers who have already shown interest and can be converted into customers by sales representatives. A third different context is that of companies whose revenue is mainly generated in offline points of sale, such as restaurants and grocery stores. In this case, the sales goal of digital marketing is to attract customers to these offline sales channels.

Serve refers to those digital marketing activities that aim to provide value-added services to a customer. Broadly understood, *serve* covers all digital marketing activities that lead to a better customer experience. Among other things, the usability of a website and its ability to answer customer queries with information-rich content—such as videos, product demos, and blogs—is part of serving customers. Some of the most concrete activities are related to digital customer service, such as the frequently asked questions (FAQs) and virtual customer service (via live chat or a chatbot) on a website or social media channel that can streamline the customer encounters both during and after the purchase process. Many online services and mobile applications that are developed by companies are also important ways to serve customers as they allow the customer to get additional value by, for example, receiving personal offers, recommendations, and informational benefits.

Speak refers to a company's efforts to increase customer dialogue and customer–seller interaction through the use of digital channels. The most common ways to increase customer–seller interaction are related to customer communications via newsletters, text messages, webinars, and web conferencing, but customer dialogue can also be fostered via social media, various customer forums, and online customer feedback forms. Increasing interaction is critical, especially because it is the best way to get to know your customers' needs and problems in depth. Acquiring such customer understanding, in turn, can be seen as a cornerstone of digital marketing as digital marketing activities should be based on customer knowledge.

Many companies almost never connect with their customers, while others do so frequently, even too frequently. For example, the sports retail chain XXL sends out a promotional newsletter every day, which can be a little too much for many receivers. Also, on Black Friday people receive more marketing messages than they are willing to receive and more than they are even capable of processing. In contrast, sometimes you would like to receive more frequent messages from, for example, your bank or electricity company. The challenge is often that customers receive too much communication from unwanted sources and too little from the sources they would like to hear from more.

Listening and dialogue are key to increasing customer–seller interaction. The goal *speak* is therefore a bit misleading as the idea in increasing interaction is not primarily to talk but specifically to listen to customers. You can listen passively, for example, by reading customer feedback and following social media discussions about your business. Sometimes it is also worth building a more active dialogue, for example, by asking the customer directly, "Are you satisfied with the product you bought?", or "How has the product worked for you?" Few companies communicate too much to their satisfied and long-term customers. Digital marketing could be used more for maintaining and developing customer relationships by showing customers that you care about them.

Save refers to increasing the cost efficiency of digital marketing and represents a key driver of shifting budget allocation from traditional marketing to digital marketing. *Save* is often manifested in a firm's efforts to digitize traditional marketing. As a simple example, companies may replace paper brochures with digital brochures. More broadly, cost efficiency is also sought by digitizing the company's processes, such as developing self-service channels for customer service and sales. Examples include online and mobile banking, e-commerce, chatbots, and self-service kiosks.

When a customer is able to select and book tickets from an airline's online service, check-in via a mobile app, and print the labels they need for their belongings without assistance, it is clear that over time there will be significant savings for the airline as the customer does virtually everything for herself or himself. Equally, a retailer saves on postage costs if it moves from direct mail to email and digital newsletters. Similarly, digital advertising is typically significantly less expensive than advertising in traditional mass media, such as television and newspapers. The smaller the target group, the greater the difference. For example, if you advertise toothpaste, mass media may still be a relatively cost-efficient channel as the target audience is very broad. If, on the other hand, you advertise an industrial vacuum cleaner, close to all (if not all) of your mass advertising will be targeted at people who will never buy one.

However, the savings generated by digital marketing should never be assessed in isolation. For example, an email campaign is probably always cheaper than a direct mail campaign, but a direct mail campaign can be more productive if it significantly increases more sales than an email campaign. Correspondingly, in the example of an airline, self-service surely saves money, but if self-service were to lead to a deterioration in the customer experience and thus to customer churn, self-service could decrease productivity in the long run.

Sizzle refers to brand building and includes increasing brand awareness and improving brand image through digital means. In particular, social media have provided new ways to build a brand by interacting with the customer and other stakeholders. Influencer marketing is an example of one digital marketing tactic that often leverages the influencer's sizable and engaged group of followers in delivering a brand's message. Of course, the same idea has been practiced in traditional media with the support of media personalities, such as athletes and actors, but social media offers room for deeper interaction and relationship building.

Viral marketing is also a phenomenon related to digital marketing, where social media users voluntarily share the content produced by the company on social media. Companies can also set up brand communities where customers can have a discussion about the brand. The most successful examples are well-known global brands, like Apple and Starbucks, that have a large enough number of enthusiastic brand advocates. For example, in Apple communities, peers help other Apple users solve problems related to Apple devices and service. Starbucks, on the other hand, utilizes crowdsourcing and gathers ideas and opinions from customers for service development. In addition to big brands, brands that promote causes that go beyond making a profit for shareholders are at the forefront of engaging brand advocates. For example, the Finnish firm ResQ's mission to reduce food waste has been addressed by thousands of consumers who spread the brand's message on social media. ResQ's corporate customers are also keen to promote ResQ's brand because they are equally eager to highlight their efforts to reduce food waste by being part of the ResQ network.

The 5S typology provides a good overview of the digital marketing goals that many companies are trying to achieve. The typology does not take a position on the order of importance of the different target categories, something which of course varies according to the company in question's strategy. Ultimately, however, at least for-profit companies seek to either increase their sales (they have the *sell* goal) or improve their cost-effectiveness (they have the *save* goal) as these goals are directly reflected in the company's earnings. It can therefore be said that for for-profit companies, the *sell* and *save* goals are the end goals of digital marketing and that the *serve*, *speak*, and *sizzle* goals are, in turn, indirect goals that help a company increase its sales or improve its cost efficiency in the long run (Figure 3.1). A company will not benefit from serving customers, developing customer dialogue, or building a brand if they do not increase sales or improve cost efficiency in the long run.

Goal setting is often challenging because it is much simpler to measure the achievement of end goals than the achievement of indirect goals. This is because the end goals can be measured by objective numbers, while indirect goals are more abstract in nature and their achievement often has to be measured by subjective, so-called mindset metrics related to customer attitudes, experiences, and intentions. Although the positive relationship between indirect goals, marketing, and overall business performance has been established via countless academic studies, it can be very challenging for an individual company to measure the extent to which improvements in brand and customer experience drive sales or cost efficiency. Partly for this reason, companies tend to overweight end goals instead of indirect goals. This is problematic, because too much focus on end goals can lead to the over-aggressive pursuit of sales and cost efficiency at the expense of customer experience or the brand, leading to poor outcomes in the long term both in relation to this and also in terms of sales and cost efficiency. For this reason, in goal setting we always recommend striking a balance between end goals and indirect goals.

3.1.2   Setting objectives using SMART criteria

Now that the types of digital marketing goals have been introduced, it is time to turn our attention to setting the goals. As a basis for this, we recommend the so-called SMART criteria as they help the goal builder to formulate the goals as concretely as possible and thus guide the digital marketing operations. The SMART criteria were originally designed for use in setting business goals in general, but they are also excellent for setting marketing and digital marketing goals. The original SMART acronym as noted is based on the words *specific, measurable, assignable, realistic, and time related.*[2] Since then, countless versions of the SMART criteria have been derived, which you can read more about on Wikipedia,[3] for example. Regardless of the exact version of the SMART criteria, its basic idea is to provide a tool with which to shape goals as concretely as possible so that the goals do not remain at an abstract level and support

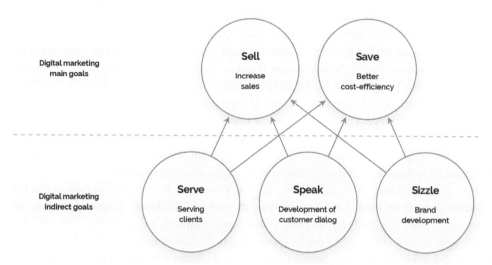

Figure 3.1   The indirect goals and end goals of digital marketing, derived from the 5S
model

a company's practical operations. In the following, we describe the SMART criteria via each
letter of the acronym.

3.1.2.1   Specific

The objective must be well defined. It is sometimes characteristic of marketing that it unnecessarily focuses on cool phrases in setting goals, such as the goal "building an innovative
frontrunner image"; it sounds great as a goal, but it can be interpreted in many different ways.
According to the *specific* criterion, the marketer in this example should first define what *an
innovative frontrunner image* concretely means. Many other marketing goals may sound
more understandable, but they may suffer from the same syndrome as the example above.
For example, *the development of customer relationships* sounds moderately concrete, but it
also does not define the development target precisely enough. *Reducing customer churn* and
increasing customer life-cycle value or customer satisfaction are examples of more definable
goals related to the development of customer relationships.

3.1.2.2   Measurable

The objective must be measurable. Otherwise, its realization cannot be verified, and in that
case, it is a vision rather than a goal. The *specific* and *measurable* criteria go hand in hand as
the choice of metrics determines what the goal ultimately means. For example, improving the
brand image is not a goal until the target brand image is defined and metrics have been selected
by which to verify how to gauge if the brand image has improved. For example, if a company's
brand image is intended to be associated with expertise and customer focus, brand research
can be used to measure customer perceptions of these attributes relative to competitors or

to take advantage of social media listening to monitor how often these attributes appear in company-related discussions in comparison with discussions about competitors.

The measurability of the goal is particularly important because it is problematic for management to focus digital marketing actions on goals that cannot be verified because then it is not possible to know when the actions are taking the firm towards the selected goals. In contrast, it is just as problematic to focus marketing actions on the goals that are easiest to measure as they do not necessarily represent the goals that are most relevant to the business. Needless to say, it is not equally easy to find appropriate metrics for all goals, but that does not mean that a commercially relevant goal should be abandoned. Indicators can be found for each objective, although in some cases it is necessary to settle for incomplete indicators or indicative indicators. Brand-related goals are a typical example of this because, while brand metrics do exist, not every company can afford to acquire comprehensive brand research in order to implement measurement. In this case, it is necessary to rely on indicative indicators, such as the reach of advertising and the organic growth of website visitors.

3.1.2.3   Assignable

The goal must be assignable, that is, a designated unit must have the responsibility for its achievement. Depending on the goal, the responsible unit may be an individual or a marketing team, or it may consist of several different teams or business functions. When there are several bearers of responsibility, it is important to agree on the division of responsibilities. For example, marketing and sales functions may be jointly responsible for increasing sales, in which case it is very important to agree on a clear division of responsibilities and roles. The marketing team may be responsible for, for example, producing leads in accordance with the agreed criteria, and the sales team may be responsible for converting the leads into deals. Sometimes it can also make sense to break down responsibilities for individuals, for example, with one marketer responsible for acquiring leads on social media and another for leads acquired through search engines.

3.1.2.4   Realistic

The goal must be realistic. It is good to be ambitious, but it is pointless to set goals that are virtually impossible to achieve. For a small brewery, for example, global market leadership is unlikely to be an achievable goal—at least not in the short to medium term—making it a dream rather than a realistic goal in the short to medium term. The realism of the goal must also take into account whether the goal can be achieved through digital marketing. For example, you might be able to double sales over a certain period of time with digital marketing, but if production and logistics cannot be scaled at the same pace, the goal is virtually impossible to achieve. The goals must therefore also take into account the realities of the business and, of course, the marketing resources and budget.

3.1.2.5   Time related

The goal must be time related, that is, it must answer the question "When will the goal be achieved?" For example, if the goal is to gain 100 new customers, in digital marketing planning, it is important to know whether it should happen in the next week, month, year, or ten years. If the time span is short, it may be wisest for digital marketing to focus on promotional campaigns. On the other hand, if the time span is long, developing a customer experience, content marketing, or brand building can be good ways to develop customer acquisition without the negative impact of promotional campaigns on margins.

According to the SMART criteria, a good digital marketing goal is therefore specific, measurable, assignable, realistic, and time related. However, the idea is not to abandon all objectives that do not meet the five criteria. Instead, the idea is to provide a tool to make an abstract goal as concrete as possible. For example, many companies state that digital marketing aims to increase customer engagement. However, *engagement* can be defined in many different ways, and SMART criteria force a company to consider what this goal means in practice and how it can be measured. The end result can be increased interaction on social media, more regular website visits or mobile app usage, a recommendation or positive word of mouth (WOM), a higher buying frequency, or something else that the company thinks reflects customer engagement. Thus, SMART criteria help to translate the marketing jargon into concrete goals and ensure that different actors in the organization understand the goals in the same way, so that they speak the same language. Even a seemingly concrete goal can be further concretized using SMART criteria. It is a different matter, for example, to set the goal of digital marketing to be "To increase sales" than it is to set the goal to be "To increase sales through digital channels by 20 percent in 2022 compared with 2021."

3.2   DETERMINING COMPETITIVE ADVANTAGE

Once the goals are set, the digital marketing strategy work will get off to a good start. Goals are relatively easy to set, while a plan to achieve the goals requires an in-depth analysis of a company's competitive advantage, that is, how the company is able to meet customer needs in a way that competitors cannot match. To determine a competitive advantage, a company must therefore have an in-depth knowledge of (1) customer needs, (2) the strengths and weaknesses of competitors, and (3) the company's resources and capabilities. A company usually knows its resources and capabilities best, so when determining a competitive advantage, the company should focus specifically on identifying customer needs and how the company's capabilities are positioned against the strengths and weaknesses of its competitors.

As a tool for identifying customer needs, we recommend creating buyer personas that take the traditional customer segmentation approach to a more individual level. In turn, the positioning of a firm's capabilities compared with the strengths and weaknesses of its competitors requires an analysis of the factors that set the firm apart from its competitors. In the following subsections, we will tell you more about buyer personas and differentiation.

3.2.1   Buyer personas

Regardless of the goals set for digital marketing, a deep understanding of the customers is the most important prerequisite for achieving them. How the goals will be achieved in a customer-centric way can only be planned on the basis of customer knowledge.

Traditionally, the marketing strategy has highlighted market segmentation and targeting that divides markets into smaller customer groups, from which the most relevant group or groups are selected as the firm's target group(s). Segmentation has typically been done on the basis of general background criteria, such as demographic and geographical criteria, that lead to segments such as 25–35 year-old women who live in Helsinki (a business-to-customer or B2C segment) or small- and medium sized central European electronics (B2B segment). There are also much more granular segmentation criteria, but the end result is always some sort of a group of individuals or companies whose purchasing needs can be very different. With digital marketing, we have moved to more and more targeted and personalized communications for which traditional segmentation criteria are ill-suited. Alongside segmentation, there is a growing need to define buyer personas that deepen our understanding of the target group at the individual level.

A *buyer persona* can be defined as an individual representing the target group of a company who has certain types of purchasing needs and criteria. A company may have one or dozens of buyer personas, but at least initially, it is worth starting with a maximum of a few of the most important buyer personas. Most often, an imaginary person, such as Simo Saver, is used as the buyer persona, but the term "imaginary" must not be misunderstood. The most certain way to fail in defining a buyer persona is to come up with the buyer persona by intuition—although it should be noted that staff often have in-depth customer information that can and should be used as part of creating buyer personas.

Buyer personas are also an essential part of brand development. The company's brand also develops based on what its customers are like. Namely, the company's existing customers attract more customers like themselves to the company. This is at the heart of branding: the company positions itself as the best option for its chosen target group. However, it all starts with creating buyer personalities and building marketing activities that suit their needs.

3.2.1.1 Creating buyer personas

Creating a buyer persona should be based on actual customer research and other data available about customers (Figure 3.2). We especially recommend having dialogue with customers—even with those who have not bought anything. Good ways to collect customer data include interviewing the company's salespeople, customer feedback and surveys, and researching customers' search behavior (e.g., by using Google's keyword tools and monitoring social media conversations).

A common mistake when creating buyer personas is that they just visualize the demographics of typical customers. Demographics do not help organizations build their marketing to support the customer's buying process. Another mistake is overreliance on web analytics metrics, such as clicks, time on site, and conversions. These metrics provide an overview of what people are doing in the digital environment but are ill-suited to creating buyer personas for two reasons. First, they produce aggregate data on people's average behavior, making the data difficult to use to identify different buyer personas. Second, they only tell you about what people are doing and therefore do not answer the question of why they are doing it.

The question "Why?" is particularly relevant to the creation of buyer personas as answering it provides a better understanding of customer needs and the motives that guide buyer behavior. Buyer personas can thus be used to find out why people behave in a certain way at certain stages of their buying process. In this way, marketing is able to steer customers in the desired direction in the purchasing process.

There are two main components to creating a buyer persona: (1) knowing the buyer persona, and (2) modeling the behavior of the buyer persona. Knowing the buyer persona is an important prerequisite for marketing to be relevant and relevant to the customer. Modeling the behavior of the buyer persona, in turn, is a prerequisite for targeting marketing activities to the customer in a timely manner via the digital channels in which the customer spends his or her time.

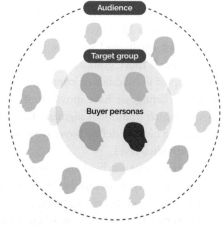

By the phrase "knowing the buyer persona," we mean that the company has a deep understanding of the broad context of the buyer's persona, that is, understanding of the customer's

Figure 3.2   Buyer personas

everyday or business problems, goals, needs, purchasing criteria, preferences, and level of product awareness. It is challenging to gain universally valid wisdom about the broad context of the buyer's persona as the broad context of the persona varies greatly depending on the company's industry, offering, and the customer base itself. However, the level of product awareness is a variable in which generalizable features can be found, and therefore we will open this up in a little more detail below.

The "product awareness of buyer persona" refers to how well the buyer already knows the product or service sold by the company. The more familiar the buyer is with the product or service sold by the company, the warmer the audience member is for marketing activities (i.e., the easier it will be to turn the customer's purchase intentions into a deal). However, there are usually a limited number of warm audience members, so it is important to also address colder audiences (i.e., buyers with a low level of product awareness), especially from the point of view of increasing sales.

The product awareness of buyer personas can be divided into five buyer categories: unaware buyer, problem aware buyer, outcome aware buyer, product aware buyer, and fully aware

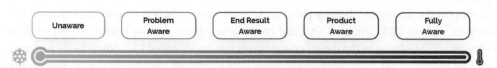

Figure 3.3   The five degrees of the product awareness of buyers

buyer (Figure 3.3). We will present the categories briefly below and explain their significance for the implementation of digital marketing.

- *Unaware*: The customer does not recognize his or her problem nor its consequences. In such a case, marketing and content should be designed so that the customer recognizes his or her problem and its consequences as this is the first step in starting the buying process. For example, a potential customer of a company focused on financial management may be a company that records travel invoices manually, which is time-consuming, but the customer does not perceive it as a problem because the process is well established. In this case, the most important task of marketing is to make the potential customer realize that its employees spend a lot of time posting travel invoices, which incurs costs for the company.
- *Problem aware*: The customer recognizes her or his problem and its effects but does not know what the solution is or whether there even is a solution. A potential customer of a financial management company may be tormented by the manual entry of travel invoices and the time wasted on it, but still does not think that there could be a solution to the problem. In such a case, the focus of marketing and content should be placed on the problem experienced by the customer and its consequences. The more accurately the problem and its effects are described, the easier it is for the customer to identify with the situation described and the more likely the customer is to believe that the company understands his or her situation. In digital content, therefore, the most important thing is to first show an understanding of the customer's problem and only then sell her or him the solution.
- *Outcome aware*: The client knows the end result she or he wants but does not know how she or he can achieve it or it feels too hard to achieve it. For example, a customer may know that the posting of travel invoices can be largely automated but is not very familiar with the solutions involved or their implementation seems too laborious. In such a case, the focus of marketing and digital content can be on what the automation of travel-invoice posting requires in practice or how simple it is to implement a solution provided by a company.
- *Product aware*: The customer knows the product (or service) but does not think it is right for him or her. This situation may be caused by the customer's previous bad experiences, word of mouth about the product or service, incorrect beliefs, excessive pricing, or poor website content. The cause must be identified and corrected. If the cause is a high price, the problem experienced by the customer should be magnified and the benefit of the product or service should be attractive and easy to achieve.
- *Fully aware*: The customer knows the product or service and wants it but has not purchased it. Reasons for this can be, for example, the website of the product or service provider is difficult to use, poor ordering instructions, the customer's lack of initiative, or the fact that the customer does not consider it important to purchase the product or service. In these situations, purchasing should be made as easy as possible and the importance of purchasing should be concretized with the help of digital content that appeals to the customer.

The level of product awareness also has a significant impact on how the customer's purchasing process takes shape. If the level is high, the purchasing process can proceed directly from identifying the need to evaluating alternatives or even making the purchase decision; if the level of product awareness is low, the purchasing process often progresses slowly and the customer may spend a considerable amount of time searching for information.

Modeling the behavior of a buyer persona allows us to take a closer look at what the customer is doing during the buying process, such as seeking out information to support her or his purchasing decision or comparing different options. With the help of modeling, digital marketing is thus structured in such a way that the activities support the decision-making of buyers.

In Section 2.3, we discussed the customer's purchasing process and the changes brought about by the digitalization of its various stages, namely, awareness, the information search, the evaluation of alternatives, the purchasing decision, and post-purchase behavior. In the following, we will explain in more detail how the steps of the purchasing process should be taken into account when creating a buyer persona. When buyer personas are created according to the stages of the purchasing process, the personas visualize how the customer's purchasing process is progressing and what things the customer is thinking about at any stage of the purchasing process and with what people. Similarly, the marketing process can be designed to support customer decision-making. When buyer personas are known, marketing becomes truly customer-centric and does not feel like an intrusive sales talk but a customer-friendly service.

3.2.1.2   Awareness

At the beginning of the purchasing process, the customer becomes aware of a purchase need that may be related to a problem, goal, or desire. The key questions in creating a buyer personality follow:

- What are the customer's needs and the motives behind them?
- In which situations do the customer's purchasing needs arise?
- How can the customer's purchasing needs be aroused?
- In which digital channels does the customer spend time?

It is important to understand the nature of the needs of different customers, as well as the situational factors that give rise to purchasing needs. Situational factors can be related to a momentary emotion (such as pain, hunger, boredom, and despair) or an event (such as the breakdown of a device, an action by a competing company, or the emergence of new technology). If a customer has a low level of product awareness, they may also have an unconscious need to make a purchase. For example, someone may hate vacuuming but still spend many hours a week vacuuming because she or he values cleanliness at home and is unaware of robotic vacuum cleaners. On the other hand, the customer may have heard of robot vacuum cleaners but doubts their quality and has therefore not sought further information on the subject. In such situations, it is especially important to identify the marketing angles with which the customer's need to purchase is best aroused in order for the purchasing process to begin.

The more complex a company's product or service is, the more carefully the purchasing needs of buyers need to be determined so that they can be aroused with appropriate marketing angles. In addition, it is important to know which digital channels customers spend their time on so that they can be reached on those channels. For example, one prefers spending leisure time on news sites, another on social media, and a third on mobile games.

3.2.1.3   The information search

Once the customer is aware of a purchasing need, he or she begins to actively seek out information in order to meet the need. The key questions in creating a buyer persona are the following:

- From which sources does the customer look for information to support her or his purchasing decision?
- Which keywords does the customer use to search for information?
- What is the customer's expertise in relation to her or his purchasing need?

There can be significant differences between customers in terms of which channels they seek information from and what sources of information they value. Search engines are by far the most typical information search channel, but there are other digital channels as well. For example, some people propose questions on social networking services and forums in search of others' opinions. Some also turn to influencers or read peer reviews of a product or service. When using search engines, customers can also use a variety of different keywords and thus end up with different sources of information.

The nature of an information search is significantly affected by the customer's expertise in relation to his or her purchase need. If a customer feels familiar with the options that meet his or her purchasing needs, the information search and keywords used will often target specific brands, products, and product models, as well as their pricing information (e.g., the "new iPhone offer"). On the other hand, if the customer does not feel that she or he is an expert and the purchasing situation is complex, the information search and keywords used by the customer may be much more general (e.g., "utilization of artificial intelligence in the financial sector"). From a marketing perspective, it is essential to understand what information customers are looking for, from what sources they are looking for it, and with what keywords they are looking for it in order to design marketing content and keywords to suit their search queries.

3.2.1.4   The evaluation of alternatives and the purchase decision

After searching for information, the customer has narrowed down the set of options to a few competing products or services and is now starting to evaluate the options in more detail in order to make a purchase decision. The key issues in creating a buyer persona are the following:

- What criteria does the customer use to make a purchase decision?
- What are the barriers to buying?
- Who else influences the purchase decision?

Purchasing criteria are the factors on the basis of which the customer ultimately chooses a product or service. There can be a wide variety of criteria, but most typically they are related to price or quality. Quality can be related to the product or service you buy or to a more comprehensive customer experience. Competition is often fierce, and it is difficult for the customer to objectively compare the price–quality ratios of products. In this case, the decisive criterion may be a factor related to the customer experience, such as active contact with the customer, a clear offer, or some other factor that facilitates the purchase decision.

In addition to purchasing criteria, it is important to identify barriers to making a purchase that prevent trade from taking place. These may be related to a missing feature in the product or service, or poor communication, for example. Sometimes there is not enough information about the product to make a purchase decision or there are uncertainties about the product's delivery fee or return policy. Barriers to buying are often simple in nature, but they still create uncertainty for the customer and quench their enthusiasm for making a purchase decision. Therefore, it is important to find out what kind of barriers to making a purchase the customer has and why the barriers have become barriers to making a purchase.

Also, the purchase decision is not always personal as more than one person can participate in making it. A new house, bathroom renovation, or holiday resort choice are examples of such multi-person purchase decisions. In the case of firms' procurements, having more decision makers is more the rule than the exception. The size and composition of a company's so-called purchasing group varies depending on the size of the company and the type of procurement. If the procurement is critical to the business, such as the purchase of a new factory or an ERP[4] system, dozens of individuals can be involved in the purchasing group. On the other hand, when it comes to purchasing new ballpoint pens for an office, there are not many decision makers in the purchasing group.

The more complex and significant the procurement, the more important it is for marketers to outline the people who influence the purchase decision and their role in the purchase process: Who identified the problem and the need to buy? Who started driving the matter? and Who was involved in the final decision? From a marketing perspective, it is important to create content that addresses each person who makes a purchase decision in the right way. For example, the Chief Financial Officer may be interested in the cost of acquiring new software, while the Chief Information Officer may be interested in integrating software with the company's information systems infrastructure.

3.2.1.5 Post-purchase behavior

The customer has purchased a product or service and switched to using it. The key questions in creating a buyer personality are the following:

- What factors affect the value experienced by the customer about the product or service?
- What kind of support does the customer need to use the product or service?
- What makes the customer recommend the product to others?

The purchase decision is ultimately based on the value the buyer believes they will receive from the product or service. Indeed, marketers tend to promise customers the value they want from the product the most. When a buyer switches to using a product, she or he compares his or her user experience to the value promised to him or her. If the product meets or even exceeds the customer's expectations for perceived value, the experience is positive, making the customer more likely to buy from the company again and also recommend it to acquaintances.

Creating a buyer persona is largely focused on the pre-purchase stages of the buying process. However, it is equally important to understand the factors that affect the value a customer experiences with a product or service. It is especially important to know what problems the customer may face when using the product or service and how he or she can be supported so that he or she can get the most out of the product or service.

The more complex the product or service, the more critical this so-called aftercare is. For example, if new software has been sold to a customer but its implementation is tedious, the customer experience can be poor, even if the software itself is excellent. In this case, the marketer should provide a better guide or provide personal support or training for the implementation. The most effective form of marketing is people-to-people recommendations, and the company cannot get them without investing in customer relationship management. It is also important to identify the phase of the customer's purchasing cycle (e.g., when the customer is planning the next purchase). This information can be used to schedule new sales efforts.

Without defining and knowing the buyer personas, the angle of marketing efforts can be completely wrong. The wrong approach does not support the customer's buying process but tries to penetrate it by force. Once the purchasing process of buyers is known, marketing can be built around this purchasing process to support buyer decision-making. In this way, marketing helps the customer solve the problem he or she is experiencing and leads him or her towards the goal he or she wants, such as experiencing pleasure. For this reason, buyer personas are the heart of the entire marketing entity and are also the strategic backbone of the MRACE® model discussed in Chapter 5.

3.2.2   Differentiation

Differentiation refers to a company's ability to set itself apart from its competitors. Differentiating from competitors is important because it gives the customer a reason to buy from the company. By differentiating itself from its competitors, the company is thus able to attract desired customers. On the other hand, differentiation also gives some of the target group a reason not to buy, which can be just as good. Why? Each company has certain customer personas in its customer base that the company is best able to serve in the entire market. If a company is able to acquire customers that reflect its ideal buyer personas, customer loyalty, company reputation, and profitability will improve. The best way to engage customers is to get the kind of customers the company can best serve.

Differentiation can be seen as an alternative competitive strategy to cost leadership, where a company strives to be the most cost-effective player in the market and thus offers customers lower prices or earns higher margins on the products it sells. However, aiming for cost leadership is rarely an ideal strategy as it increases price competition in the industry, decreases margins, and degrades service quality and employer image. It therefore also makes it difficult to create sustainable competitive advantages as it is usually easy for competitors to imitate cost reductions. However, aiming for cost leadership remains a typical strategy in industries where products or services are very homogeneous and therefore difficult to differentiate. For example, for raw material producers and electricity companies, differentiating themselves from competitors is considerably challenging.

Differentiation requires a critical analysis of a company's similarities to and differences from its competitors. In addition, which differences are relevant to the customer and how they are communicated to the customer as clearly as possible must both be considered. Differentiation therefore always requires knowledge of the buyer personas and the competitive landscape.

At its weakest, a company's attempt to stand out is blunted into a circular slogan. These include "good service," "competent experts," "long industry knowledge," "extensive experience," or "a customized turnkey concept." The problem with these slogans is that they concretely say little to the customer, and they often represent basic expectations in the customer's eyes. What else can a customer expect from an expert service than skilled experts, and long and extensive experience, tailored to their needs? Another weakness lies in the fact that often many competitors also try to stand out with exactly the same slogans, so that none of the competitors clearly stands out from others. A company must therefore have full knowledge of the competitive field in order for differentiation to be possible at all. It is hard to stand out if you do not know from what you are standing out.

For example, a premium coffee machine brand, Moccamaster, would hardly cost €100 more than a "regular" coffee machine if they were to advertise it with the phrase "You can get coffee at the touch of a button in just a few minutes—just add water, filter paper, and ground coffee. Designed by top experts!" Instead, Moccamaster communicates about the coffee experience and the perfect coffee, where the time the water passes through the ground coffee is calculated just right so that the customer always gets perfect-tasting filter coffee. The product is also different in appearance from other filter coffee machines, which is part of the storyline.

On the other hand, even if a company finds a very concrete way to differentiate itself from its competitors instead of using a fuzzy slogan, the customer may not perceive it as relevant. For example, a company may stand out from its competitors with a new cool logo, but its significance to the customer may be negligible or non-existent, meaning it does not affect the potential customer's purchase intention or existing customer satisfaction. Every business is unique, and it is easy to come up with a differentiator. In turn, it is often difficult to find a differentiating factor that is relevant to the customer. The unfortunate thing is that a considerable amount of time and money may be spent creating differentiating factors that are irrelevant to the customer. For example, there are a huge number of business-created mobile apps in the world that are hardly used by anyone.

The differentiating factors that are relevant to the customer are those that are not offered by other companies and that are valued by the customer. Creating buyer personas is key to identifying relevant differentiating factors. With customer-relevant differentiation factors, a company can ask for a higher price for its product, engage its customers better, arouse the customer's desire to buy faster, increase the attractiveness of its brand, and even completely stand out from the competition as a category above the market. Differentiation does not always mean that a product or service needs to be clearly better than its competitors or better than them at all, it just needs to be packaged and communicated in the right way so that it exactly addresses the desired audience.

We next go through five key ways in which a company can differentiate itself from its competitors. Some of these are things that can be implemented relatively quickly, and they relate to marketing communications and brand image. On the other hand, some are more fundamental things that require transformation to the whole business. These include creating a new category for the market, product focus, and customer focus, which we will introduce first.

3.2.2.1 Creating a new category for the market

Companies can differentiate themselves from their competitors by adapting quickly to changes in the market, but the clearest way to differentiate themselves from competitors is to reshape existing markets by creating an entirely new category in the market. In this case, the company effectively withdraws from price competition. If the product is in a completely different category, why compare it with others?

A simple example of creating a new category for the market is Tesla, which can be considered to have introduced a completely new category in the car market for electric cars. Initially, Tesla withdrew from price competition, and it took a long time for competitors to enter the competition. Another example is HubSpot, which launched not just one new marketing automation system but a whole new way of doing marketing, Inbound Marketing. This is how HubSpot stood out from all other marketing automation systems, although technically it is very similar to all the other leading systems.

Creating a new category is, of course, a difficult, expensive, and long-term task that requires real professionalism from the entire company. The new category is not created in the blink of an eye and requires excellent productization and a story in the background. If successful, it will create a strong differentiating factor for the company.

3.2.2.2 Product centricity

Product-centric companies focus on making the best product on the market, trusting that customers will buy the product because of its excellence. The challenge with this model is that the features of products and services are often at least somewhat replicable, despite possible patents. Consequently, the brand also has a strong role in product-centric companies. An excellent example of a product-centric company is Apple, which strongly focuses on developing its products so they are better for their target audiences. "The best" is always a relative concept, and no product can be the best for everyone. Apple has focused a lot on the ease of use, design, appearance, and unique features of its products.

3.2.2.3 Customer centricity

In customer-centric companies, customer service and customer experience are at the heart of everything. This can be reflected in the features of the product, as well as in the daily operations of the company's employees. For example, Netflix is a very customer-centric company as their services are different for each customer based on, among other things, their viewing history. Another example is the online shoe store Zappos, whose growth, especially in the early stages of the company, has been due to high-quality customer service and the elimination of all risks from the customer. Zappos offers free shipping, a 365-day money-back guarantee, and 24-hour customer service every day of the year. According to Zappos, the longest customer service calls have lasted as much as 11 hours as they are dedicated to solving customer problems.

3.2.2.4   Brand appearance

A unified brand appearance can differentiate a company from its competitors. Few people buy a product or service just because of the brand appearance, but a unified look creates recognizability, a quality image, and thus, also trust. Trust, in turn, plays a key role in generating sales and customers. Coca-Cola is one example of a brand whose visual look has remained very consistent over time, inspiring confidence in the minds of customers.

3.2.2.5   Marketing communications

Brand appearance is what the company looks like. *Marketing communications*, on the other hand, are largely what a company sounds and feels like. Distinctive marketing communications focus on sharing useful information rather than telling customers about the excellence of a company or its products. Would it not be more comfortable to take your child to a kindergarten that would concretely tell you on their website how the child's first day is planned and how the child is included among the other children rather than take your child to one that says their kindergarten is full of educational professionals, has good customer-oriented service, and many years of experience?

3.3   VALUE PROPOSITION AND VALUE CREATION FOR THE CUSTOMER

Once a company has a deep knowledge of the needs of its buyer personas and has identified the factors that allow it to differentiate itself from its competitors, it will be able to determine its competitive advantage. The company therefore knows how it is able to satisfy the needs of its customers in a way that competitors cannot match. However, even a clear competitive advantage will only become a real competitive advantage if a company succeeds in communicating it to the target group in a way that is memorable. Therefore, the company must be able to communicate the core of its competitive advantage in such a way that the customer understands what value the company can create for him or her (i.e., why he or she should do business with that company). This translation of competitive advantage into a form that is understandable to the customer is called *a value proposition* and should guide the core messages of marketing, regardless of tactics, channels, or campaigns.

The difference between competitive advantage and value proposition can be illustrated by the following example. The competitive advantage of an airline may be that it is able to provide its services more cost-effectively than its competitors. Through this competitive advantage, it is therefore able to either offer the customer lower prices or sell flights with higher margins, provided that the quality of the service is not significantly lower than that of its competitors. Competitive advantage, on the other hand, could be translated into very different value propositions depending on whether the company wants to increase its sales at lower prices or improve its profitability with higher margins. An airline could translate the competitive advantage of cost-effectiveness into, for example, the value proposition "we offer cheaper prices than our competitors" or, more specifically, "our prices are always at least 1 percent cheaper than the second-cheapest prices." If a company does not want to engage in aggressive price competition and prefers to focus on maximizing margins, its ability to communicate a clear value proposition to the customer is significantly reduced. Partly for this reason, the value propositions of many companies are full of beautiful and abstract words that do not necessarily mean anything at all, such as "we provide sustainable service in a customer-centric manner."

In addition to low prices, a company's value proposition can focus on the quality and range of products and services sold, the experiential or smooth flow of the customer experience, or more generally, the core benefits that the company offers to its customers. A good value proposition highlights a company's differences from its competitors, addresses the needs of buyers, and concretizes the value the company offers. One clear value proposition is better than ten unclear value propositions. You may have noticed smartphone ads that mostly advertise the device's excellent camera, even if the phone has more computing power than the laptops of a few years ago. This is precisely because one concrete promise of value goes much further than telling customers about all the possible good things about a product. The more value propositions and marketing angles that are highlighted, the duller and less effective they become.

A value proposition should be drafted carefully as it has a significant guiding effect on the operational level of marketing—every marketing action should live and breathe the value proposition you choose. Therefore, an airline that emphasizes its low prices in its value proposition should not focus on promoting comfortable seats or having pleasant staff on the aircraft as the aspects do not communicate the value and strength of the image of being the cheapest airline on the market. The sole purpose of the marketing by such a company is to reach those who want to get from Place A to Place B as cheaply as possible and to convince them that the airline is indeed the cheapest.

However, adhering to marketing actions in line with the value proposition can also pose challenges for the company. If there are very different buyer personas, creating a unified and clear value proposition can produce difficulties. For example, many brands and retailers have value propositions that relate to customer centricity, sustainability, and digitalization while their marketing communications focus on price promotions that do not reflect the chosen value proposition. Companies should therefore remember that providing something for everyone is often the same thing as providing nothing for anyone and they should primarily focus on the firm's key buyer personas when making a value proposition. With a clear value proposition, a company is able to differentiate itself from its competitors, create unique value for its target group, and be the best single option in the entire market for the needs of its chosen buyer personas.

Humorously, it has been stated that the deepest essence of marketing is crystallized in the slogan "Overpromise and underdeliver," which suggests that corporate marketing communications often promise too much and these promises are too often unfulfilled. In order for a value proposition not to remain fuzzy buzzwords, the company must carefully plan how the value promised to the customer is created in the day-to-day operations.

3.3.1 Value creation strategies

Value creation for the customer is the core of the entire customer-centric business—a company only creates value for its owners when customers are willing to pay for the value they create. From a digital marketing perspective, value creation emphasizes how a company is able to leverage data and technology to create value for customers. In digital marketing, three key value creation strategies can be identified that create value for the customer and the company in slightly different ways: (1) targeted and personalized marketing, (2) a superior customer experience, and (3) value co-creation (Figure 3.4). Next, we will deal with these one by one.

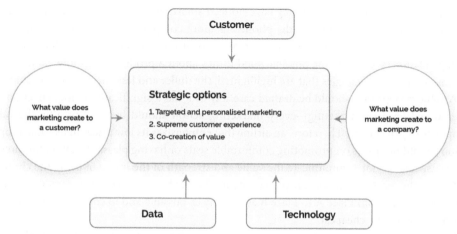

Figure 3.4   Value creation strategies

3.3.2 Value creation strategy 1: targeted and personalized marketing

3.3.2.1 The objective

Targeted and personalized marketing is a value creation strategy that aims to deliver the right marketing message to the right customer, in the right place, and at the right time. Although targeted and personalized marketing has taken place since the early days of direct marketing, the potential of the strategy has exploded in the digital age as digitalization provides firms with significantly more diverse data on customer behavior that can be leveraged for more accurate targeting and personalization. In this context, *targeting* means that a particular marketing action, such as an advertising message or offer, can be targeted at the buyers who are most likely to be interested in it. Similarly, by *personalization* we mean that we can tailor the content of the message or offer with a specific buyer in mind.

3.3.2.2 The means

The means comprise highly targeted digital advertising and communication, personalized product recommendations, benefits, and offers.

3.3.2.3 The value to the customer

The value of targeted and personalized marketing to the customer is based on the idea that a well-targeted message is a service. When successful, the idea is easy to agree on—few of us get upset when, for example, we get an offer for a product we are currently looking for. Unfortunately, there are probably more examples of failed targeted marketing than there are of successful ones. Of course, this does not mean that targeted and personalized marketing is a bad strategy; it means that putting it into practice is not always easy. On the other hand, the irrelevant advertising messages we encounter every day also tell us that a large percentage of companies do not even try to be relevant; many do digital marketing like mass marketing, pushing messages into different channels without an idea of who might be interested in them.

3.3.2.4 The value to the business

Targeted and personalized marketing brings value to businesses in the form of better productivity as it both increases sales and reduces costs if successful. The more relevant the message, the more likely it is to grab the customer's attention, stay in her or his mind, and get her or him to act in the way the company wants (e.g., they want him or her to make a purchase). On the other hand, better targeted communication directly reduces costs because, for example, the advertising budget is no longer wasted on making unnecessary impressions. Of course, it must be mentioned that well-targeted and personalized communication requires the support of know-how and technologies, the acquisition and implementation of which require financial investment.

3.3.2.5 Who it is for

Targeted and personalized marketing is basically suitable for a wide variety of companies that strive to streamline their marketing communications and make them more relevant to customers. It is especially suitable for online retailers or other companies with a large number of different products or services, a large number of customers, and a lot of data-accumulating touchpoints between the customer and the company. This is because targeting and personalization are done in a data-driven manner, and thus, the more data that is collected from different customers and their touchpoints, the more accurate the targeting and personalization can be. In addition, the implementation of the strategy is supported by the company's analytical expertise as targeting and personalization are largely based on analytics-based behavioral data. Marketing automation and machine learning are technologically the solutions that increase the economies of scale of targeting and personalization.

3.3.2.6 A practical example

An extreme example of a successful implementer of this strategy is Amazon, which has hundreds of millions of customers, many of whom regularly use Amazon's online services. From these digital meeting points, Amazon accumulates a huge amount of data that it can use to personalize product recommendations and other relevant communications based on automation and machine learning.

However, the Amazon example does not mean that targeted and personalized marketing could not be implemented with smaller customer numbers and touchpoints. In particular, the targeting of communications can be successful even if there are few customers. Personalization is also possible with a small number of customers, but in this case, the scale advantages brought by personalization are reduced or, alternatively, the accuracy of personalization suffers.

3.3.3   Value creation strategy 2: a superior customer experience

3.3.3.1   The objective

The goal of a superior customer experience is to support the customer throughout the customer life cycle. At the heart of the strategy is an in-depth understanding of the customer's problems and goals, which the company must be able to address with content and services that benefit the customer. Building buyer personas is therefore an essential foundation for achieving a superior customer experience. Because maintaining a customer relationship in most cases involves both physical encounters and digital encounters between the customer and the company, a superior customer experience requires the successful integration of digital marketing into the marketing, sales, and customer service processes. Thus, a superior customer experience is not a separate value creation strategy for digital marketing but digital marketing plays a growing role in digitizing customer encounters.

3.3.3.2   The means

The main role of digital marketing is to build a streamlined or smooth purchasing process. In practice, this means directing the customer towards the purchase by answering the customer's questions through content marketing and enabling a low-threshold contact with the company (e.g., through a chat service) when the customer needs advice. Even after purchase, it is important to provide an easy channel for customer service and to respond quickly to problems encountered by the customer. A superior customer experience also involves ensuring that the customer receives the maximum value (i.e., the maximum benefit or enjoyment of the product or service they purchase). This can be supported through content marketing and various digital services, such as mobile applications. For example, the benefits of smartwatches are quite limited without the additional digital services associated with them.

3.3.3.3   The value to the customer

A better customer experience saves the customer time when shopping and helps the customer achieve goals and solve problems. Post-purchase support helps the customer get the most out of the product or service they purchase. Of particular importance to the customer experience is that problems encountered by the customer after purchase, such as delayed delivery or quality defects, are solved promptly. A prompt response to problems is at the heart of customer focus.

3.3.3.4   The value to the company

Good customer experiences lead to customer satisfaction, loyalty, and recommendations. These are of great importance to the long-term success of a company. Although the development of the customer experience should not, in principle, be considered from the point of view of cost-effectiveness, a good customer experience can at best lead to customers acting as the company's best advertising channel, which can also reduce the need for paid visibility.

Likewise, a good customer experience reduces angry phone calls to customer services and thus also brings savings. On the other hand, customer service personnel need to be well resourced so that customers do not have to queue to solve their problems. For example, Zappos' customer service staff are instructed to talk to customers for as long as the customer wants to talk about something, such as fashion trends. The idea is that a company should always have time for its customers. This embodies a customer-centric mindset and is far from the following typical ways in which we measure the effectiveness of customer service staff: how many calls a customer service agent manages to receive per hour, how many problems he or she manages to solve in that time, and how much additional sales this generates.

3.3.3.5 Who it is for

A good customer experience benefits every company providing such an experience, but the strategy is best suited to companies that (a) seek to differentiate themselves from competitors by other means than price and (b) have an offering that represents the so-called high-involvement category, which requires at least some degree of planning and reflection from the customer. Such an offering is related to broader problem solving, such as the purchase and adoption of a new device, which means that the customer has to spend more time and energy in making a purchase decision and learning how to use the product or service they are buying. In this case, supporting the customer during and after the purchasing process will play a more important role than it does in routine-based purchases, such as when purchasing a milk carton.

To succeed, a strategy requires an in-depth understanding of the buyer personas and their purchasing processes. The company needs to understand the customer's information needs and critical encounters during the purchasing process as they determine the formation of the customer experience. From an internal point of view, this requires the organization to embrace truly customer-centric thinking in all of its operations, which is often a long process and something that is not just in the hands of the digital marketing team. In terms of data, a superior customer experience requires qualitative data about the buyer and, on the other hand, behavioral data from different touchpoints in the purchasing process. The use of technologies, in turn, is determined by which technological solutions create value for customers and thereby improve their experience.

3.3.3.6 Practical examples

An excellent example of a superior customer experience for a potential customer is provided by the American company called Sungevity, which provides customized solar energy solutions for households and commercial properties. Their main idea has been to build such a compelling and value-creating customer journey that the customer would not even think about competing alternatives. From the customer's point of view, the path to purchase is described step by step as follows:[5]

The customer receives a direct-mail letter titled "Open this to find out how much your family can save on energy costs with solar panels." The letter includes a personalized URL that leads to a Google Earth image of the customer's house with solar panels added. The next click leads to calculations of energy costs that take into account the average energy costs of the household, as well as the estimated number of panels that can fit on the roof and the angle of the roof relative to the sun. The next click will lead to a conversation with a sales representative who can see the same images and calculations. The sales representative provides the customer with more information and sends her or him links to videos that explain the installation process in detail.

A couple of days later, Sungevity will send customer references from the surrounding area with their contact information. When such a customer next contacts a sales representative, the representative knows exactly what stage the customer is at in the buying process and is able to make an offer immediately. The offer is emailed to the customer who can sign it digitally. When a customer returns to the website, its home page is personalized to show the progress of the customer's ordering process, and alerts are also sent to the customer's email about the progress. After installation, Sungevity regularly informs the customer about the energy and savings generated by the panels.

While this Sungevity example focuses on a superior customer experience in the pre-purchase phase, Glaston,[6] in turn, provides a great example of a superior customer experience in the post-purchase phase. With the consent of its customers, Glaston collects global sensor data on how customers use the glass-processing machines and technologies sold by Glaston. Based on the data, they provide customers with a cloud service that helps them improve machine efficiency, reduce emissions, and save on energy costs.

In addition to sensor data, Glaston utilizes machine vision to monitor the quality of the glass produced and to report quality defects. In the development phase, there is an application that investigates the causes of quality errors so that, for example, the maintenance needs of the machine can be reacted to faster. Glaston also offers a free machine-based mobile app that can be used to test the safety of glass. The company's future goal is to build an AI solution that makes recommendations for glass-processing recipes and, ultimately, automates all glass production.

Through the actions described above, Glaston will be able to bring tangible benefits to customers, such as energy savings and better-quality end products. Indeed, marketing often devotes too many resources to measures aimed at acquiring new customers. The example provided by Glaston is a good reminder that the customer's path to purchase is only the beginning of the customer experience. The superior customer experience is not limited to the shopping experience but deepens as the customer relationship develops.

3.3.4   Value creation strategy 3: value co-creation

3.3.4.1   The objective
The goal of value co-creation is to engage customers and/or other stakeholders in solving problems that are relevant to all parties. At its simplest, a strategy can mean engaging customers to develop or customize offerings for them. More broadly, such a strategy can mean that a company is part of a larger ecosystem or network that aims to create value for the actors involved in the ecosystem. A company can either strive to create new ecosystems or become part of an existing ecosystem. Value co-creation is not purely a digital marketing strategy, but it has significant implications for the implementation of digital marketing. At the heart of

value co-creation is not targeting, personalization, or even the customer experience on digital channels—at its heart is a digital dialogue between a company and its customers and partners.

3.3.4.2 The means

The means include digital communities and innovation platforms, crowdsourcing, social media listening, and dialogues on digital channels.

3.3.4.3 The value to the customer

In the value co-creation, the customer is not an object but an active subject in developing the offer to suit himself or herself and/or finding solutions to social problems. Thus, in the value co-creation, the communication is not tailored to the customer, but rather, the product or service concept itself is tailored to the customer. The customer may thus have a significant influence on the value offered by the selling party. In many cases, it is not so much about a seller–buyer relationship but a real partnership in which a new innovation or solution to a business or social problem is built together.

3.3.4.4 The value to the company

Cooperation with customers and partners helps to identify new business growth opportunities and the emergence of new innovations, offerings, and business models. In addition, the customer's involvement in value creation, such as offering development and customization, increases the likelihood that he or she will also find it useful. Cooperation between a company and a customer also often results in customers acting as messengers of the company's brand story.

3.3.4.5 Who it is for

Value co-creation requires, above all, strong and confidential customer and stakeholder relationships. Indeed, value creation is typically at the heart of digital marketing in B2B industries, which often have a smaller number of strategically significant customer relationships. The seller and the customer are often partners whose business relationship is not based on the transaction but on the parties' ability to benefit from each other's business. In this case, in digital marketing, the main focus is on building a dialogue between the parties.

3.3.4.6 Practical examples

At best, value co-creation is about solving a relevant problem. For example, on Unilever's website[7] it lists challenges related to sustainable development, health, and other important themes that they are committed to addressing for a better future. On their site, they invite stakeholders to develop solutions related to the themes and provide an easily accessible innovation platform on which to propose ideas and solutions. On the consumer side, crowdsourcing is fairly common among large brands. For example, My Starbucks Idea is a well-known example of a crowdsourcing platform where Starbucks gathered thousands of ideas from consumers for product and service development and implemented the best of them.

Value co-creation works best for companies when the company's customers commit to the messengers of the brand story. This is only possible if the company is able to build a brand that makes the customer care about the brand (i.e., the customer creates emotional ties to the brand). Indeed, there is talk in the brand literature that brand building should move from storytelling to meaning making. A relevant brand means that a company generates benefits to society that go beyond paying taxes, that is, it solves environmental problems or corrects social disadvantages.

NOTES

1. Chaffey and Smith (2017).
2. Doran (1981).
3. Wikipedia (2021).
4. ERP: Enterprise Resource Planning.
5. Edelman and Singer (2015).
6. Mero, Karjaluoto, and Tammisalo (2021).
7. Unilever (2021).

PART II
IMPLEMENTING MARKETING STRATEGY IN PRACTICE

4
Implementing strategy using the MRACE® model

In the second part of this book, we will look at how to implement a marketing strategy created based on the previous chapters. As we stated at the beginning of the book, we use the MRACE® model that was launched by Suomen Digimarkkinointi as the guiding model for this book. Once a company has developed a marketing strategy and a value proposition based on a competitive advantage and once it has clarified its goals based on these, the task of the operational part of marketing is to create a competitive advantage that accelerates the company's growth. At its best, the operational implementation of marketing generates enough daily traffic to the company's website and daily leads that it keeps the sales team's contact list of potential customers growing. In addition, the operational level of marketing produces softer results in the long run, such as awareness and brand development. All this can be achieved through marketing according to the MRACE® model. What is the MRACE® model and where did it come from? Let us go through the answers to these questions next.

4.1   WHAT IS THE MRACE® MODEL?

One of the best-known names in digital marketing is Dave Chaffey, who has developed one of the most widely used digital marketing models (see Smart Insights). The name of the model is RACE, which comes from the words *reach*, *act*, *convert*, and *engage* (Figure 4.1). The RACE model is described as a so-called sales funnel, and although it is more than a decade since its launch, it is still a widely used digital marketing model across industries.

The RACE model begins with planning, which creates a comprehensive digital marketing strategy that includes goals and a plan for achieving them. We discussed this in the first part of our book. The first step in the model, Reach, means creating awareness. Creating awareness

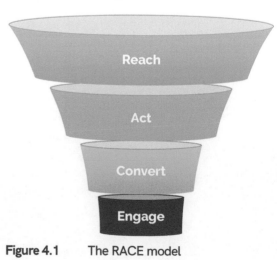

Figure 4.1   The RACE model

is related to awareness of a company's brand, products, and services. The goal is to direct visitors from elsewhere on the web to the company's online content.

The second stage of the model is Act, which is an abbreviation of *interact*. The Act phase means creating leads from the perspective of sales processes. Typical interactive elements of the Act phase include signing up as a loyal e-commerce customer, adding products to a shopping cart, viewing a product page, downloading a buyer's guide,[1] attending a webinar, reading company blog posts, liking and sharing content on social media, and subscribing to a newsletter.

Convert refers to *conversion*: purchasing in the context of the RACE model on either a digital channel or an offline channel. In the Convert phase, the main task of marketing is to convert a lead into a ready-to-sell lead through marketing automation and/or getting the customer to request a quote. The task of marketing is also to support sales in closing the sale by targeting the person requesting the offer, for example, by placing references to closing the sale in various channels.

The last step in the model is Engage. In digital marketing, *engaging* means building a long-term customer relationship using digital channels. Most often, this means newsletters and social media, that is, the digital channels that committed customers use when interacting with a company.

The MRACE® model is based on the RACE model, but MRACE® underlines performance measurement as a crucial part of each phase of the RACE model (Figure 4.2). Only by measuring digital marketing can it be continuously developed to be more effective. Thus, the MRACE® model will guide the continuous development of digital marketing and the testing of new ways of improving results. Continuous testing and development are important not only because of profit development but also because they enable digital marketing to adapt to a constantly changing operating environment, such as that resulting from changes in customer behavior, technologies, and channels.

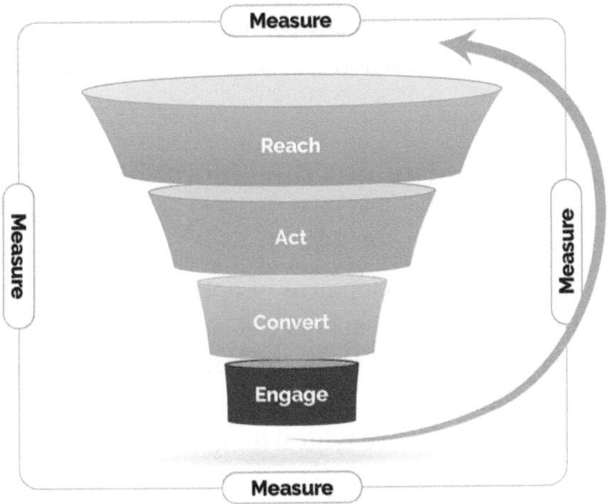

Clear and flexible models like the MRACE® model help companies evolve and move towards digital sales and business. Currently, digital commerce is reshaping all businesses in all industries faster than ever and no slowdown is in sight. The speed of change has meant that many companies lack a model suitable for today's needs upon which they could base the development of their marketing and sales in a systematic and measurable way. In addition, with the continuous development and growing number of digital platforms, the challenge has been to serve customers both agilely and profitably. A clear model

Figure 4.2   The MRACE® model adds a fifth phase to the RACE model: Measure

improves the understanding of how changes and development actions in marketing affect the whole marketing process.

The MRACE® model is based on the idea of multi-channel marketing, and turning multi-channel marketing into a measurable entity is the main goal of the model. In this case, each channel and marketing tool works to its full potential in the marketing process with the channels and tools supporting each other. Although different digital channels and marketing tools are suitable for many uses, each channel and tool still has its own clear place and goals: digging with a tape measure is slow and using a shovel for measuring is impractical. When each marketing channel is only used for the purpose to which it is best suited, marketing becomes a seamless and effective whole without the channels being siloed.

The MRACE® model has four significant benefits when looking at the operational performance of marketing across the enterprise. First, the model guides action as it visualizes the entire marketing process in a single image, making it easier to manage. When challenges are identified in marketing, they do not raise questions but trigger action.

Another significant benefit is that the model makes marketing inherently very customer-centric. The model is used to build marketing around the buying process of the buyer personas. In this way, marketing is integrated as a natural part of the customer's purchasing process and does not remain a separate and pressing part of the process.

The third benefit is that the model transforms marketing into data-driven marketing. Only by measuring and analyzing the data can the right actions be taken in order to develop marketing. In addition, the model directs the focus of marketing so that the best-performing actions are invested in and the weakest are developed or omitted. As the fourth benefit, the model simplifies marketing management. The model connects different channels, prevents them from being siloed, and allows marketing to be directed in the desired direction. In this way, marketing is focused on the right things, and the focus does not shift onto thousands of new-sounding marketing tricks and technologies.

Although the MRACE® model is extensive, it integrates with any company and strategy due to its straightforwardness and universal nature. Its introduction also does not require a great deal of implementation, only a change of mindset.

4.1.1   The MRACE® model and the continuous development of marketing

Marketing must be developed not only because of the development of operating profits but also because the world is different today. Customers are moving to new social media channels, so advertising will no longer reach them, competition will intensify, buying behavior will change, trends will evolve, and content will get outdated. Therefore, the MRACE® model is never fully complete but guides you to constantly look for two critical things:

1. What factors *slow down* the return of marketing investments?
2. What *improvements* will lead to the greatest improvement in operating profit?

The whole of marketing is only as strong as its weakest part. For this reason, each step of the MRACE® model is set with its own performance metrics (KPIs), according to which marketing is continuously developed based on data. KPIs make it possible to assess at an early stage whether the set targets are being met. For example, if a company wants to make ten trades a month and if each trade requires 1,000 visits to be directed to the company's site, measuring the number of visitors is a good KPI metric. If your website has only received 2,500 visitors by the middle of the month, the goal is likely to be missed because it requires 10,000 visitors to your site in a month.

The principles of the model are thus very similar to those of *growth hacking*, which consists of setting goals and making hypotheses, analyzing the actions, and drawing conclusions based on data (Figure 4.3). With the conclusions, new goals and hypotheses are set when the cycle, the so-called development print, returns to the beginning. One development print is typically short in duration and predefined. Continuous improvement, data integrity, and rapid experimentation are at the heart of the operation.

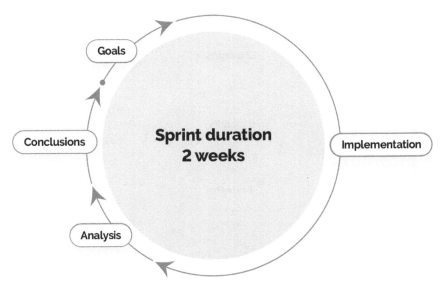

Figure 4.3   A two-week development print that consists of four steps (setting goals, implementing them, analyzing the results, and drawing conclusions), after which the sprint will start again with new goals

It is easy to talk about continuous development and quick daring experiments, but implementing them in reality in a busy day is challenging. Activities need to be planned and carefully structured because otherwise they will only remain at the level of speech and things will not be implemented—or if they are implemented, their impact on business will easily remain a mystery if data is not collected and analyzed.

Agile methods form an excellent tool with which to support this kind of marketing that aims for continuous improvement as we live in a complex world where a large part of the cause-and-effect relationship can only be noticed in retrospect. In reality, most marketing is just an expert's best guess as to what measures could be taken to get the best possible result. It is therefore impossible to fully predict the market and the behavior of people. Thus, the sooner cause-and-effect relationships are found in the market and in people's behavior, the faster the outcome of marketing can be developed.

Agility, growth hacking, and growth marketing may be reminiscent of a bunch of super-creative people who develop the craziest ideas where only the sky is the limit. Crazy ideas can be good, of course, but every idea and development print should be based on the long-term goals of the organization.

It can be thought that today's actions determine whether an organization will achieve its goals over a longer period of time. If there are no clear goals and strategies behind the agility, being agile will lead somewhere in the long run, but probably not to where one wanted to go (Figure 4.4).

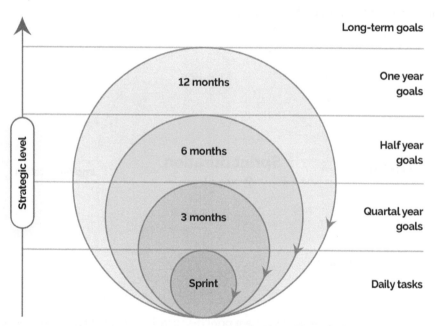

Figure 4.4   Daily tasks should contribute to long-term goals

4.2   THE STAGES OF THE MRACE® MODEL

At this point, you should have a clearer idea of what the MRACE® model is and what its stages are. Next, we will delve into each individual step in more detail in order to get an idea of what tools and channels work at each stage of the model. You will also learn about the typical challenges of the steps and how to solve them. We present the instruments of digital marketing in more detail in Chapter 5.

4.2.1   Reach

As we said earlier, the Reach phase is about creating awareness (Figure 4.5). The goal of this phase is to make the target audience aware of what the company has to offer and direct relevant traffic to the company's website. The Reach phase begins when a message reaches a potential customer and ends when the customer visits the website. Thus, in the Reach phase, the largest possible flow of visitors according to the buyer personas is directed to the site from the different digital channels by communicating to them in the ways defined in the strategy phase. At this point, potential customers falling within each buyer persona can be roughly divided into three different segments:

Figure 4.5   The Reach stage

1.   Customers actively searching for the product
2.   Customers searching for a similar product
3.   Customers who are not searching for the product but would benefit from using it.

A *product* also means a service. The following example illustrates the segmentation of potential customers: Imagine you are selling oat milk. In this case, customers in the first segment are specifically looking for oat milk, customers in the second segment are looking for some kind of milk to put in their coffee, and customers in the third segment are not looking for any kind of milk.

These segments can be reached, for example, through search engine marketing (see Section 5.3) and social media marketing (see Section 5.5). There are two practical ways to actively search for a product on the website of the company selling the product: searching for it from Google Ads advertisements or from the organic search results that appear after the sponsored ads on the search engine, thanks to search engine optimization (SEO). Sure, it is possible that someone searching for the product will come across an ad for a product on social media, but if they are currently looking for a particular product, the most likely first contact will be through Google.

Those looking for a similar product are not looking for a product offered by a particular company but are generally looking for a solution to their problem. So, for example, a customer is only looking for some kind of milk to put in their coffee—be it made from oats, soy or made by cows. In such cases, it is possible to target your advertising to different audiences on different advertising platforms on Google, Facebook, Instagram, and LinkedIn.

For those who are not looking for a product but would benefit from it, it is most effective to advertise through Google's Display and Discovery networks, as well as through social media channels. Of the social media channels, in Finland, Facebook is usually the best (even for a B2B target audience) because it is the most-used social media channel. Advertising on YouTube is also a good way to increase awareness. Through Facebook, the target group can be communicated to about the challenges or needs they experience. When a member of the target audience identifies himself or herself in an ad post, his or her attention is earned and he or she can be directed to the site to read more about the topic. In the content of the site, his or her need to solve the problem is translated into a desire to buy just the product offered by the company. In the example of milk for coffee, the ad could start with the question "Do you always burn your tongue when you drink coffee?" or "Does your morning coffee taste too bitter?"

The most common problems in the Reach phase are that a company's potential customers do not know how to search for a product and the company's website is not found by search engines when the customers try to find the product. If the customer does not know how to search for a product online, the solution is to place the product in front of him or her. This is mainly done by advertising on social media, YouTube, Discovery, and Display. However, this is not always enough as the customer may not know that he or she needs the product in question. In this case, the advertising should communicate the end benefit of the product or the problem that the product solves. If, on the other hand, the website's search engine visibility is poor, it needs to be improved. This is done through both SEO and search engine advertising. You can read more about these in Section 5.3 ("Search engine marketing").

4.2.1.1   The role of the brand in the Reach stage

A brand is a rather difficult thing to measure and verify, which is why there are many different opinions about its importance in marketing. A brand can be a name, a term, a symbol, a person, or any attribute that differentiates a product or service from others. When talking about brands, it is generally thought that a brand is well known and evokes positive associations in the minds of customers. Indeed, the customers' perceptions and mindsets ultimately determine what a brand really is. Because a brand is a subjective view, some well-known brands will be completely unknown to some. For example, China's best-selling car brand is a strong global brand and a well-known brand worldwide: Volkswagen. On the other hand, the most-purchased Volkswagen model in China in 2019 was the Lavida, which is not a brand for Finns because Finns have probably never heard of it.

However, a brand is known to have a clear impact on marketing performance as it can increase trust in the company. Of course, the impact of a brand can also be negative if the brand has a bad reputation. However, it can be said that companies with a strong brand do not have to use their resources in marketing to tell them *what* they are doing. Instead, they can focus on telling you *how* they are doing it. For this reason, we will go through each step of the MRACE® model to see how important the brand is to the performance of each step.

A brand brings the following three benefits in the Reach stage:

1. A brand brings leverage and increases awareness. The brand image is much emphasized in the Reach phase. If all of the company's ads look visually consistent, each ad will enhance the audience's memory footprint of the brand. For example, in social media, the same person sees the same ad or its variations multiple times.

2. A brand increases the consistency of advertising. When the brand image and the tone of the company are consistent and carefully thought out, the company appears unified and consistent to its customers. You can compare this to a restaurant visit: If the first waitress who serves you is friendly and helpful and the second is rude and bored, it is hard to say which of these represents the restaurant's standards, leaving the image of the restaurant in the dark.

3. A brand increases confidence. When a brand is strong, there is no need to build trust between the brand and its customers from scratch. In this case, the company also does not have to use its resources to build trust nearly as much as a company with a weak brand. A new airline company may need to assure you that they are reliable and that their flights are safe. In contrast, Finnair, for example, does not have to tell its customers about the reliability of its flights, the professionalism of its personnel, or that the customer will be able to get to their destination with their help as we Finns know Finnair's long history and solid experience in flying. With a strong brand, a company's Reach phase advertising can focus more on customer needs rather than building trust in the brand.

4.2.2   Act

The Act (i.e., a shortening of *interact*) stage begins when the information seeker arrives on the website and ends when the visitor becomes a ready-to-sell lead (Figure 4.6). The main goal of the Act phase is to turn a website visitor into a lead. Exceptions include companies for which building a brand and attracting customers is more important than acquiring leads. This is the case, for example, with most food companies.

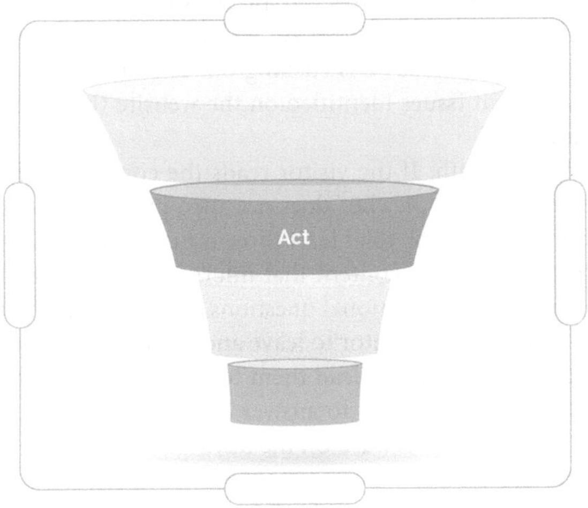

For those businesses that need to generate leads and demand through their website, the Act stage is the most crucial step in the entire MRACE® model. If it fails, there will be no sales opportunities. At the heart of everything is the technical functionality of the website and conversion optimization (i.e., optimizing the usability of the website to make it easier for the customer to request a quote or make a purchase; see Section 5.3.1). The traffic generated during the Reach phase will not turn into leads without a purchase path created by

Figure 4.6   The Act stage

the content or a well-functioning website.

When the overall content offering that has been created forms buyer persona-specific purchase paths, they lead the acquired traffic to take the desired actions, such as downloading a guide, and make microconversions, which are small measurable activities that give an indication of a person's interest in the company. A microconversion can be, for example, reading a blog article from start to finish. With the help of a consistently designed purchasing path a single visitor will spend more time with the brand, reading or viewing more content (such as blog articles, customer stories, or videos). This presupposes that each content item creates an interest in reading or watching the next content item, otherwise the visitor's path to purchase will stop. The more content a visitor gets to read or view, the more he or she learns about the products and services on offer and the more he or she becomes convinced that he or she should buy a product from that particular company and not from a competitor.

4.2.2.1   Problems of the Act phase and their solution

The general challenge for companies in the Act phase is that while traffic to a site can be obtained, it does not turn into leads or requests for quotes. In this case, it should be determined whether visitors (a) spend time on the website or (b) leave it quickly.

Scenario "a": The visitor spends time on the website but does not turn into a lead.

There are roughly four reasons for this problem:

1. The website is slow and does not work properly technically or in practice. In this case, the best solution is to use SEO and conversion optimization together. SEO ensures that a website is fast and that it works correctly technically. Speed and technical performance have a big impact on search rankings so the website is ranked better in Google search results. Conversion optimization helps ensure that traffic on the website is unobstructed. It pays attention to, for example, the number of prompts, the length of the forms, and the analysis of the text structures, as well as to how the buttons are placed on the page. The so-called heatmap tools (see Section 5.3.1) show what each visitor is doing on the website, what section the visitor is browsing, and what she or he is clicking on. The end result of conversion optimization is an analysis of what issues identified on the website (based on customer behavior) are worth correcting.
2. Content does not create a consistent buying path. If the visitor reads the content to the end (i.e., if he or she is clearly interested in the topic) but does not turn into a lead, the buying path will leak. Each item of content must link to at least three other content items so that the customer's buying path continues to the content that interests them most. It often happens that the content of a website raises additional questions for the visitor, but he or she cannot find the answer. This will cause the visitor to leave and search Google for an answer to her or his question, which will most likely lead them to a competitor's site. So, there needs to be a lot of content on the site in order to answer all the questions that concern the customer and thus guide the customer forward on the buying path.
3. Leads are not acquired aggressively enough. If a visitor is not redirected to the desired action from each content item, the visitor will not become a lead. Lead acquisition can be improved by improving the landing page (the page to which a person is directed through advertising). Usually, the landing page has some specific goal, such as getting the customer to download something, attend a webinar, or contact the company. In addition to improving the landing page, lead acquisition can be made more efficient by creating time- and behavior-based pop-ups. Facebook's Lead Ads ad format is also a great way to get leads as it allows a potential customer to download the guide directly on Facebook by entering their email address in the field provided on Facebook. The more downloadable content a website has based on buyer personas' drivers, the more leads are obtained, even if the

website's traffic does not increase at all. For example, a company selling garden products could make downloadable guides for sowing a lawn, caring for a flowerbed, and removing weeds from an entire yard. The more specific the topic of the downloadable guide, the better it meets the needs of a particular target group, which will increase the interest of the target group and increase the number of downloads of the guide.

4. The customer is not returned to the website through remarketing. The customer's purchase path is not linear, and the customer leaves the website even though he or she is interested in a guide or considering requesting a quote. None of this may seem appealing to the customer at that very moment (e.g., due to urgency or fatigue), so he or she leaves it for later. However, it is likely that he or she will not remember the topic later, in which case he or she should be redirected back to the website through remarketing. The best ways to get the customer back on their buying path are through remarketing on social media, Display, and YouTube. Email marketing is also a good way to remarket if the customer has previously subscribed to a newsletter, for example.

Scenario "b": The visitor leaves the site quickly and therefore does not turn into a lead.

This problem is typically caused by three things:

1. The traffic directed to the website is incorrect. If paid advertising targets and communication angles are not created based on buyer personas, marketing often becomes too circumspect. In that case, it will reach more people but the people it reaches may not be the best people for the business. The first step is to adjust the targeting and messaging angles of social media and Google ads in order to match the buyer personas so that the right people can be reached with the right message.
2. The content is bad or inconsistent with the advertising message. We live in the midst of a constant flood of information flow. If the content of a company's website does not arouse our interest immediately, we will not read it further and will leave the website. Therefore, all content should be built on the basis of buyer personas so that it is fully focused on the customers outlined in the buyer personas and on solving their problems. Talking about a product alone does not interest anyone in general, but the fact that a company talks about customer problems and how to solve them is of interest to most customers.
3. The website loads slowly. If your site is slow, your immediate bounce rate will always be higher than normal. According to research, every tenth visitor leaves a website immediately if the page loads for more than two seconds. If the download time is seven seconds, the number increases to one in three visitors.

4.2.2.2   What kind of website content is needed for the Act phase?

The content of articles encountered at the beginning of the buying path plays a key role in the Act phase, ensuring that the customer is interested in reading more articles and moving forward on the buying path. If the content only tells customers about the product itself, it will only address a target group of people who already want to buy the product. This group is usually quite small. Instead, the content at the beginning of the buying path should focus purely on the customer. They should address her or his problems, needs, goals, and day-to-day challenges according to the buyer persona. The more accurately customers are described, the more likely they are to think that a company will be able to solve their problems.

At the beginning of the buying path, customers search for information on search engines with need-based, problem-, and motivation-based search terms or phrases such as "How do I generate leads?" or "The car makes a weird sound when it starts." If the content provided by the company only deals with the company's products, the company will not be found in the search results with such motive-based keywords. The keywords used by customers should therefore be clarified with dedicated tools such as keywordtool.io.

Let us take an example of how motive-based content can trigger the buying process. The sales director of the company enters "How can I improve the closing percentage of salespeople?" in the search box of the search engine. He ends up with the content "This is how you can improve the salespeople's closing percentage through marketing," where he is taught why a poor closing percentage is not always due to salespeople and that it can also be due to poor quality leads, for example. The sales manager gets interested and continues to read. He is directed to the content "Generating Quality Leads for B2B Companies." In this article, he finds the downloadable content "Modern Sales Manager's Toolkit: 37 Tools to Streamline Your Sales Process and Improve the Quality of Your Leads." The sales manager downloads the guide and the company that created the guide receives the contact information of the sales manager (who is their potential customer) and can thus send him emails with marketing automation before contacting him.

4.2.2.3   The importance of the brand in the Act stage

In the Act phase, the customer begins to map out where she or he could buy the product or service she or he wants. Dozens of companies can take part in the competition, and in this situation, it is important to stand out.

A well-built brand offers the following three benefits in the Act phase:

1. The brand sets the company apart from its competitors. A brand is perhaps the best way to stand out from the competition because it cannot be copied. In contrast, the features of a product or service, website purchasing paths, the content of a website, and the angles of advertising can be copied. Of course, differentiation itself is already a strong way to brand a company.
2. The brand creates interest in the company. You are more likely to be interested in and trust in someone who is nice and consistent. The same applies to companies, and consistency and making a good impression should be quickly communicated to customers at all points of contact between the company and the customer, whether the points of contact are physical or digital. A brand that looks interesting will increase the amount of time visitors spend on the brand's website. Thus, potential customers spend more time with the brand, which makes them more likely to commit to the brand.
3. The brand appeals to the company's dream customers. With a well-built brand, the company arouses interest in the target groups and customer groups that it wants as its customers. Such customers are more satisfied and profitable, take less resources from the company (e.g., in the form of handling complaints), and attract more customers like them to the company.

4.2.3   Convert

The Convert stage includes the time when the visitor is a lead but not yet a paying customer (Figure 4.7). At this stage, the main task of marketing is to convert the lead into a ready-to-sell lead with marketing automation and/or to get her or him to ask for an offer, and to support sales representatives in closing the deal by offering, for example, customer references to the person requesting the offer.

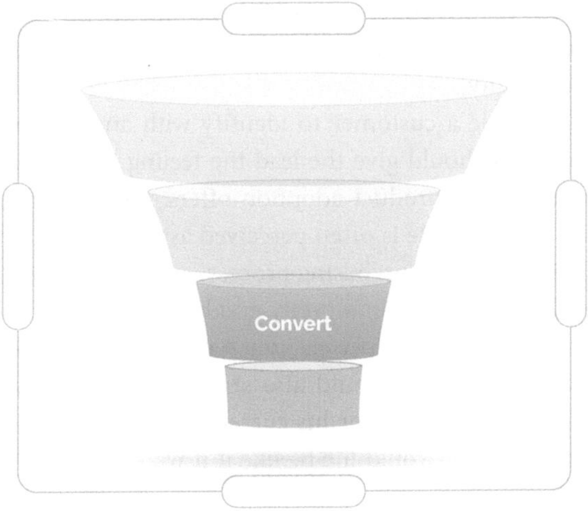

Figure 4.7   The Convert stage

The nature of the Convert stage varies greatly from industry to industry. In some products, the biggest responsibility in converting a lead into a deal lies with the sales representatives, while in others the responsibility lies with marketers. For example, buying windows for a house is difficult for many without the help of a sales rep, while Software-as-a-Service (SaaS) systems are often purchased completely independently.

Multi-channel digital marketing is important because the customer's path to purchase is not straightforward. Before requesting a quote, a customer may visit a company's website multiple times, subscribe to a newsletter, search for information about others' experiences with the company, and compare the company with its competitors. The duration of the process ranges from days to years, depending on the product: for example, consumers may take a long time to consider kitchen renovations and B2B customers may take a long time to consider a new ERP system, while milk and copy paper are purchased quickly, often fully automatically and routinely. You can think of any relatively expensive purchase you make. How often have you immediately bought a sofa or car recommended by a seller from the first store you visit when you have not familiarized yourself with the market offerings in advance? The majority of people are afraid of making mistakes and want to ensure that they find the optimal product or service for their needs.

In the Convert stage, one of the most effective ways marketing can support sales is to promote your company's customer testimonials and case examples to leads or quote requesters through remarketing on social media and Google's Display and Discovery networks. In this way, the company stays in the customer's mind and at the same time convinces her or him of its competence. If a customer has sent several invitations to tender to different companies, reference stories that the customer can identify with will make a significant contribution to closing the deal. Another good way is to create a series of emails for the marketing automation system that are automatically delivered to the people who have requested a quote. Depending on the industry, marketing automation can help, for example, justify a purchase to other decision makers in the organization, tell reference stories, and list common mistakes when purchasing a product. With SEO, you should make sure that your business is well matched with the keyword "[Company X] experiences," among other search queries.

4.2.3.1   What kind of content does the Convert stage need?

In the Convert stage, the lead is already clearly interested in the company's product. The customer must therefore be convinced of why he or she should buy from that company and not from a competitor. This decision can be supported by customer testimonials and case studies that go through a successful collaboration between the company and the customer in the form of a story, buyer's guides to help the customer make a good purchasing decision, and content that showcases the expertise of the selling company.

The contents of the Convert stage must enable a customer to identify with and remove barriers to making a purchase. In addition, they should give the lead the feeling that she or he wants the future that the benefits gained by the product adoption offers. Humans tend to seek for convenience, so a "pretty good" current state is often perceived as a better option than time-consuming information retrieval and a long purchasing process, even if these were to make us better off in the end. So, we would rather lie on a pretty good couch than spend our time and energy looking for, buying, and carrying the perfect couch up to the fifth floor and taking the old couch away. Therefore, the content should also strongly communicate what happens if the person does not make a change to her or his current state. What issues are caused by lying on an old, good couch, and what would life be like if it were replaced by a perfect couch?

4.2.3.2   Convert-stage problems and their solutions

There are two common problems with the Convert stage:

Problem 1: Leads are not converted into deals. In this case, the problem is (a) the quality of the content or (b) the sales process.

Content-quality problems often occur when, for example, a buyer's guide is downloaded a lot but very few downloaders convert into customers who make a purchase. However, judging by the number of downloads, the content in question is of interest to the customer base, so only the quality of the downloadable content needs to be improved. At its best, downloadable content paves the way for the first conversation between a customer and a seller. The content provides a lot of useful additional information to the customer, but at the same time, it has to make the customer's current state feel bad compared with the future state the company offers. When a seller contacts the downloaders of such content, a large proportion of those who read the content are sales-ready leads.

Problems in the sales process can be, for example, technology or people oriented. The wrong technology, such as a poor CRM system or the complete absence of such a system, make the day-to-day work of sales slower and more difficult. An example of a people-driven problem, on the other hand, is making too slow responses to requests for quotations. If a customer urgently needs a product, she or he often chooses the provider who is the first to respond to her or him and whose service and price match her or his criteria.

Problem 2: There are too many leads. Due to there being too many leads, the sales department is unable to focus on their best leads with sufficient resources. If you have a lot of leads, you should focus on marketing automation, conversion optimization, and content marketing.

With marketing automation, the company's most relevant and sales-ready leads from masses of leads can be directly filtered to the sales team. Conversion optimization and content marketing, in turn, can be used for attracting the sales-ready leads in order to make a request for a quotation so that the initial stage of the sales process requires less effort from the sales team. Conversion optimization removes all technical barriers from the customer's purchase path, making it easier to submit a request for a quotation. Content marketing improves the quality and quantity of content so that it resonates with the sales-ready leads, making them more willing to request a quotation.

4.2.3.3 The importance of the brand in the Convert stage

In the Convert stage, it is time for the customer to make a purchase decision. A strong brand has already had a positive impact on the customer in the Reach and Act phases, so these phases also have a relevance to converting the leads into deals. In the Convert stage, however, the following two things are heavily influenced by a strong brand:

1. The company does not need to prove its excellence. Well-known brands like Adidas or Nike do not have to prove that they are good at making running shoes because everyone already knows that. Therefore, in the Convert stage such companies can focus their marketing and content-production resources on things other than content that is purely intended for gaining trust. In contrast, the situation is completely different for less-known brands.
2. A strong brand makes purchase decisions emotional. You may have experienced this yourself: You are buying a product that requires moderate judgment. You know that Option A has slightly better features and is even a little cheaper than Option B. You still buy Option B because it feels like a better decision. This often happens, for example, in the acquisition of smartphones. The flagship model of a new and unknown brand can be superior in terms of features and price, but many times, a consumer still ends up purchasing an iPhone because it feels like a risk-free option. Thus, a strong brand increases the desirability of the product and reduces the desirability of competitive offerings.

4.2.4 Engage

The Engage stage begins when the lead becomes a paying customer (Figure 4.8). The goal of the Engage stage is to get hard-earned customers to commit to the company as it is much easier to sell to existing customers than it is to sell to new ones, and at best, they also act as brand advocates and referees for the company. In addition, the sustainable business growth comes from high customer retention and low customer churn.

The nature of the Engage stage varies greatly from industry to industry. For example, in the software business, customer engagement begins immediately through a so-called onboarding process, during which the customer learns to use the new software and gets the benefits he or she needs from it. In the service business, the service itself plays the greatest role in fostering customer engagement.

In simple terms, marketing in the Engage stage leads the customer to use the product more often and better. The best ways to do this are remarketing on social media, Google, and YouTube, and email marketing. At the heart of it all, however, is search engine-optimized content to which the customer is directed through the channels mentioned above. When SEO is well designed, visitors are steadily attracted to the

Figure 4.8 The Engage stage

content from day to day, even if you do not invest any money into your marketing. Carefully designed marketing in the Engage stage has another benefit: it helps in acquiring new customers by increasing the confidence of leads and site visitors in the company. They find that the company takes good care of its current customers by guiding them in the use of their product or service.

Engagement is often only considered to start after the first purchase, and we have placed the Engage stage in the MRACE® model in the post-purchase phase. However, customer engagement can be fostered from the beginning of the purchase process. Engagement before the actual Engage phase is nurtured through positive experiences on the path to purchase and through brand image. Creating a compelling path to purchase, brand building, and engaging customers are therefore not separate activities and must be taken into account in all marketing activities.

Learning to use a new product often feels cumbersome. We easily get excited about the features of the product at the purchase stage but forget about them in everyday use. Therefore, customers should be reminded of how they can make better use of your product or service. Using even the smallest detail of every product or service commits the customer to the company better. If a competitor's product does not have a feature that the customer has become fond of, the threshold to switching to competitive offerings will increase.

Actively sending emails to the entire customer base also increases the likelihood that customers will commit to the company. However, there are differences between industries and products regarding what things a company should communicate to its customers. The customer is presumably more interested in hearing about the products related to her or his hobbies from her or his seller rather than, for example, getting information on a monthly basis from their electricity company about how to save electricity or how the electricity she or he buys is produced. It is not advisable to send the same mass message to the entire customer base; the content of the message should be tailored on the basis of the products and services that a given customer has purchased. In that way, the message is more relevant to each recipient, which makes the messages more valuable to him or her. This, in turn, makes customers more receptive to the messages and more willing to act on them, attitudes that are reflected in higher open and click-through rates of messages.

4.2.4.1 The importance of the brand in the Engage stage

In the Engage stage, the brand's role is to get more customers to commit to the company more strongly. The impact of a brand is created in the Engage stage with very little work if the previous stages have already created a consistent brand image. In the Engage stage, it is important for a company to communicate in line with its brand image (i.e., to use the same tone of voice and continue its customer-embracing attitude) so that the customer experience remains just as good after the purchase as before it.

The brand brings the following benefits in the Engage phase:

1. Customers are more engaged with the brands that fascinate them. With the help of the brand, the company has attracted its ideal customers and they have become real customers. The best way to engage customers is to initially acquire customers whose problems the company can solve. In addition, the brand has a big impact on how strongly these ideal customers engage with the company. Commitment is really important for business predictability and profitability as high commitment means high customer loyalty, even in difficult times. During the toughest times of the COVID-19 pandemic, you may have been wondering how your favorite brand or restaurant will survive and how you could support them. If so, the companies you thought of were probably the ones to which you had an emotional connection.
2. A fascinating brand is more likely to be recommended and talked about. Referral is one of the most powerful forms of marketing. Referrals are not directly controllable, but a fascinating brand increases the likelihood that customers will recommend it to their acquaintances because brand engagement turns customers into fans of the company and this is reflected in how they talk about the company.
3. Customer churn is reduced. Stronger customer engagement in itself reduces customer churn, but an emotional connection to the brand increases a customer's willingness to forgive mistakes. All companies sometimes make mistakes: the product was defective, the customer service representative had a bad day, or someone simply made a clear mistake. If the customer has no emotional connection to the company that made the mistake, his or her perception of the company easily becomes negative. If, in turn, the company has a strong brand, the customer knows what the company represents, what its normal performance level is, and is engaged with the brand and one or two mistakes will not drive the customer to a competitor. So, a strong brand is more easily forgiven.

4.2.5   Measure

In digital channels, everything can be measured, which offers a lot of opportunities for marketing development (Figure 4.9). At the same time, however, it also creates big risks. The amount of data is easily overwhelming, and the wrong numbers can distract you. In addition, the quality of the data is very often poor, so interpreting it can even lead to erroneous conclusions. Measurement should not only be done for the joy of measuring; measures should be planned to be company and channel specific. What metrics tell us today that a company is moving towards its five-year goal? In addition, it is a good idea to look critically at selected metrics from time to time as the business evolves when sales and market processes evolve.

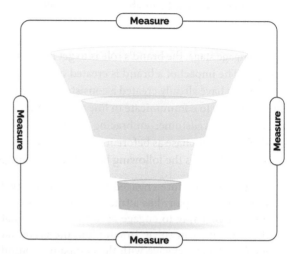

When measuring the results of marketing, it is important to consider the big picture. Good or bad results for a single channel or a single MRACE® model phase may not move sales up or down. Therefore, it is important to ask yourself what the development in a particular channel ultimately affected or will affect. Is increased website traffic reflected in increased requests for quotes? Will paid advertising produce as good a result if its cost is reduced by 30 percent? Will the leads from a new,

Figure 4.9   The Measure stage

very successful campaign turn into transactions, or will the leads from that campaign be completely useless? Marketing is often blinded to its good results and forgets to engage in a dialogue with sales, in which case improvements in marketing results may not be reflected in increased sales.

We have compiled the most important metrics to measure for each step of the MRACE® model and outline them below.

4.2.5.1   Reach-phase metrics

Reach-phase metrics are always selected on a case-by-case basis, according to the business. The most common metrics for the Reach phase are the following:

- The number of new website visits
- The total number of website visits
- A higher placement in Google's search results and the number of brand searches
- Social media reach
- Cost per click (CPC) and cost per mille (CPM; the cost per thousand impressions).

The Reach phase measures the reach and cost-effectiveness of advertising and the number of visitors to your website. However, the Reach-phase metrics require a lot of further interpretation as the affordability of advertising or the increased traffic to your website alone can appear to be big disadvantages in the Act-phase metrics. For example, if low-cost website traffic has been completely irrelevant and visitors are not even the company's target audience, they will leave the website quickly and the end result is only increased total advertising costs.

So it is worth considering whether the traffic you get is relevant, whether your site has risen higher in Google's search results (when using important search words), and whether cheaper advertising has yielded at least the same number of results as before or whether the results have dropped in relation to the costs. Interpreting the results of the Reach phase is made easier by looking at the metrics in the Act phase that tell you about visitor behavior on your website.

4.2.5.2 Act-stage metrics

In the Act phase, the quality of the traffic received is measured. In addition, indicators that look at how to improve visitor flows can be considered. For example, if visitors who come to the website through a particular advertisement spend a lot of time on the website, you can try giving that advertisement even more visibility.

Typical Act-stage metrics include the following:

- The time visitors spend on the website
- The bounce rate
- The exit rate
- Scroll depth
- The pages visited
- The number of products that visitors added to their shopping cart
- The number of newsletter subscriptions
- The number of downloaded guides
- The price per lead
- Engagement in social media posts.

The indicators of the Act phase tell a lot about the quality of the website traffic gained, as well as the functionality and ease of use of the website and the interest in it. If a visitor on the website spends an average of just a few tens of seconds on the site, the bounce rate is high, and the visitors are not turning into leads, then the traffic you get and the content on your site are not likely to be in line; your visitors are looking for something other than what the website offers them.

Find out which channels, campaigns, and search keywords drive the highest-quality traffic to your website. What content do visitors read and is certain content read for longer than other content? Things like this tell a lot about what interests your customer base.

4.2.5.3 Convert-stage metrics

The most important measure of the Convert phase is to track how much profitable revenue is generated by the visitors you acquire. Typical metrics for the Convert phase are the following:

- The number of contacts made via forms
- The number of clicks on emails and phone numbers
- Transactions made
- Purchases
- The average order price
- The return on ad spend (ROAS).

In the Convert phase, we will start to see what kind of results the marketing has achieved in euros. While the metrics for the Convert phase are straightforward and contacts or requests for quotations can always be imagined to be good things, this may not always be the case. For example, the number of requests for quotations may be too small in size, unnecessarily burdening sales and taking up their time from key customers. It is therefore good to remember that indicators and figures always require interpretation and evaluation of their real impact.

4.2.5.4   Engage-stage metrics

Engage-stage metrics measure customer engagement with the company. Typical indicators include:

- Repurchases (i.e., customers buy more than once)
- Product recommendations
- Product reviews
- The email open rate (as a percentage) (i.e., the percentage of recipients that open the emails sent by the company)
- The number of visitors returning to the website
- The number of active customers (i.e., the number of customers the company has repeatedly invoiced).

The Engage-phase metrics also tell a lot about the success of other phases in the MRACE® model. If customers engage with the company and frequently purchase its products or services, the company has been able to acquire a customer base in the Reach stage for which the company can add value that competitors cannot. When customers commit to a company's products and services because of the value they generate, it is very difficult for competitors to attract those customers to themselves, even with clearly lower prices. Engage-phase metrics are also a good indicator of business profitability. If customers only buy once or do not recommend the company to others, the company will not be able to grow as fast as it could.

In the Engage phase, look specifically at what kind of customers buy the most, are most satisfied, and recommend the company to their acquaintances. This also provides good insight into the types of customers you want to reach with advertising in the Reach, Act, and Convert stages.

You can read more about measurement and the tools that apply to it in Section 5.6 on analytics.

CASE STUDY
CASE EXAMPLE: THE INSURANCE COMPANY VARMA DIGITALIZED ITS SALES NETWORK

Varma is a pension insurer for work in Finland whose basic task is to secure pensions. Varma takes care of the statutory employment pension security of private entrepreneurs and employees. Companies take out earnings-related pension insurance (called TyEL) for their employees, while entrepreneurs insure themselves with pension insurance for the self-employed (called YEL) insurance. Funds raised as pension contributions are invested productively and securely for both current and future pensions. The goal of Varma's marketing is to increase its market share, especially among small companies because Varma's market share is already strong in large companies.

HOW DID VARMA START TO INCREASE ITS MARKET SHARE AMONG SMALL BUSINESSES?

Traditionally, the sales network in the employment pension insurance industry has been built on intermediary insurance brokers and agents. Today, the Internet, smartphones, and digital marketing tools have made it possible to move to an efficiently scalable direct-to-consumer business model, that is, to create a direct customer relationship between a pension insurance company and a customer without intermediaries. The sales network was rebuilt where customers are, namely, on Google, social media, and Varma's website.

However, occupational pension insurance involves a wealth of detailed information that is unknown to customers beforehand, which the customers then search for independently online. This has turned Varma's mindset of marketing upside down; from Varma's point of view, the customer's purchasing process is the customer's service process. It is more important to help the customer than to just offer their products and services. With this change in mindset, the marketing process began to be made more small-business friendly.

Varma's marketing relies heavily on Google, both in the preliminary information search phase (the Reach phase) and in the subsequent purchasing phases (the Act and Convert phases). Active content production was brought to the center of Varma's marketing. Prior to that, Varma invested a lot in knowing its buyer personas and its target group because knowing the target group is an absolute prerequisite for effective content production and digital marketing. Measuring the effectiveness of marketing and the data generated by analytics made it easier to get to know buyer personas and understand customer behavior.

A FEW KEY FIGURES

REACH

With SEO, organic traffic (i.e., free traffic from search engines) accounts for 55 percent of website traffic. That is a very good figure because if Varma stopped all marketing, 55 percent of their website traffic would still be retained.

Social media reached 684,194 people in six months.

Ads placed on social media were watched over 10 million times.

ACT

The bounce rate was just 37 percent, so the traffic is very relevant.

CONVERT

Hard conversions, such as direct invitations to tender and lead volumes, increased by 106 percent compared with the previous year.

The conversion rate increased by 26 percent compared with the previous year.

ENGAGE

Returning visitors to the website account for 32 percent of the website's traffic, meaning that the website's content engages visitors well as one in three visitors return to the website.

The number of brand searches increased by 50 percent compared with the previous year, so awareness and interest in Varma increased.

NOTE

1. A *buyer's guide* refers to, for example, a 15-page downloadable pdf file in which a company gives its customers information about a topic they want to know about.

5

Digital marketing channels and tools

When it comes to digital marketing, we are constantly faced with the question of what channels and tools should be used. In the MRACE® model, different channels play a key role as marketing is largely about publishing and sharing content on the right channels. The tools of digital marketing are referred to by many names: *means, channels, instruments, tools, platforms,* and so on. Usually, however, the names all refer to the same thing, that is, the ways in which a company publishes and distributes digital content and performs other marketing and sales activities. In our book, we use the words *channels* and *tools* to also describe the publishing and sharing of content.

In this chapter, we will cover the most important tools for digital marketing and their suitability for use in the stages of the MRACE® model. The main tools of digital marketing are the company's website or service, content marketing, search engine marketing and online advertising, customer relationship management (such as marketing automation and email marketing), and social media marketing (Figure 5.1).

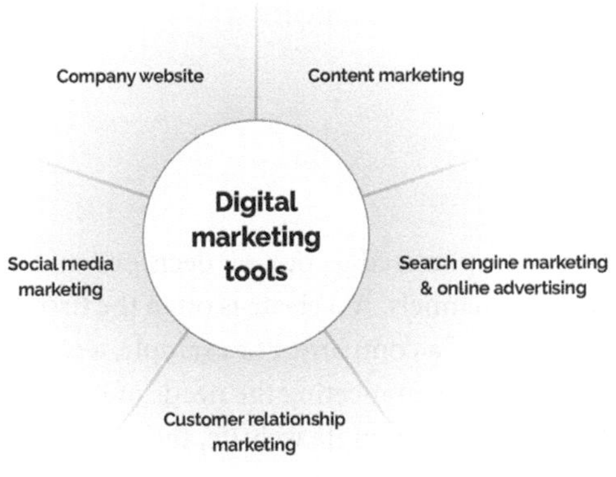

As a whole, a company's website or web service is often the most important means of digital marketing as building a digital presence begins with creating a website for the company. The structure and content of a website can only be determined once the most important question has been answered: Who is the website meant for?

Another important tool is content marketing. *Content marketing* means all the content that a company produces intended to stimulate interest in products. In this book, however, we focus on the textual content of the company's website, the videos, and the visual look of the company. With the help of content marketing, the company is able to exactly address the target groups and buyer personas they want to address.

The third key tool is search engine marketing and online advertising. These include, among other things, advertising on ad networks such as Google, banner advertising on various

Figure 5.1   Digital marketing tools

websites, and appearing on search engines (SEO) and advertising on them (search engine advertising).

The fourth key tool of digital marketing is customer relationship marketing, a subcategory of CRM, that is, marketing from a digital marketing perspective, email advertising, newsletters, and instant messaging services. Typically, all of these are related to developing an existing customer relationship when a company communicates offers or news. The goal of customer relationship marketing is to introduce and ultimately sell the company's products to existing customers.

The fifth key means is marketing on social media. Social media is a broad form of media and covers a wide range of things and channels. As a rule, *social media* refers to communities and discussion forums outside a company. The most well-known social media platforms are very familiar to most of us; Facebook, Twitter, YouTube, Instagram, and LinkedIn are the most well known and largest in terms of the number of users. In addition, in recent years Snapchat and TikTok have also gained a strong foothold as social media channels used by companies.

5.1　　A COMPANY'S WEBSITE OR WEB SERVICE

A company's website or web service is typically the basis of all digital marketing. A website usually contains at least the following:

- A presentation of the company and its products and services, with options to order them online
- References (i.e., listing a more detailed presentation of existing customers)
- Current affairs (blog, webinars, and other databank-like content)
- Links to social media channels
- Investor communications
- Analytics
- Contact information.

The importance of the website is constantly being emphasized as buying decisions and sales are increasingly taking place entirely through digital channels. A website is often the first place in which a potential customer starts to create an image of a company. For example, a company can invest a lot in the sales material of its sellers, as well as in meeting the needs of its customers, but is it evident on the company's website? If not, based on its website, the company will look worse and more unreliable than it really is. In that case, the first impression is also weaker than it could be.

It is also noteworthy that a company's website is the only digital marketing channel that the company owns in addition to a possible mobile app and an email list. Marketing channels owned by third parties, such as Google and Facebook, may change at any time and may become more expensive to advertise in, but the website will remain under the control of the company regardless of the situation. There are a few instances in history of major third-party platform upgrades: for example, Google Ads, at that time known as Google AdWords, became so much more expensive overnight with a new upgrade that many companies lost their primary source of traffic from Google as they could not afford the service.

5.1.1 The elements of a good website

The ability of a website to generate sales will be emphasized in the future as advertising on Facebook and Google, for example, becomes more common. It will lead to an increase in advertising costs as more companies compete for the same visibility. If there is no return on higher advertising costs, advertising will no longer be profitable. You can think of it along the lines that the expensive rental of a brick-and-mortar store does not hurt if the store really sells a lot; however, if there are no sales, the expensive rent is a problem. The same goes for high advertising costs in online sales—they do not hurt if a website generates a lot of leads, requests for quotations, and sales.

The elements of a website that support digital sales can be roughly divided into three sections: flawless technical functionality, appearance that creates a feeling of trust, and content created for the buyer personas (Figure 5.2).

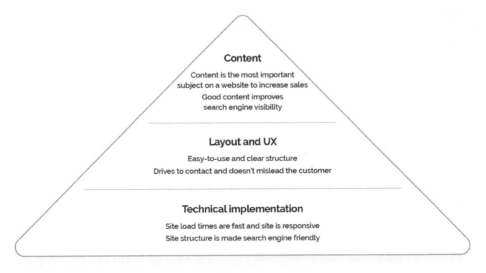

Content
Content is the most important
subject on a website to increase sales
Good content improves
search engine visibility

Layout and UX
Easy-to-use and clear structure
Drives to contact and doesn't mislead the customer

Technical implementation
Site load times are fast and site is responsive
Site structure is made search engine friendly

Figure 5.2   A website that supports digital sales

The first step is to make the website work exactly right technically. The technical implementation serves as the basis for the website because if the foundations are not in order, the website may not work well enough to maximize digital sales. The technical implementation ensures, among other things, that the website works quickly and correctly on all devices, that it is search engine-friendly, and that it enables the measurement of marketing results. If a site is not search engine-friendly, it will not show in the search results and customers will primarily only find the website through paid advertising. In this case, the advertising costs are easily higher than those of the company's competitors, but the result is the same.

A website visitor will also trust your business more when everything is working properly. What kind of picture would you have if a seller came to a meeting late, forgot some of the materials, and sent an offer a couple of days later than he promised? A similar image is transmitted from a website that is slow, where form submission does not work, and where some of the text runs off the screen when browsing the website on a mobile phone. Even if that company has the best solution for your needs, it will not be relayed from an incomplete and poorly functioning site.

In addition to technical functionality, the layout of the site must be clear so that people know how to use the site properly. A good and branded look increases trust in the company, which is especially important for first-time visitors to the company's website. A carefully planned and clear layout also communicates the company's operating models regarding whether things in the company are done somewhat in the right direction or if they are done as well as they could be.

The third element that supports digital sales is good content, which can be considered the spearhead of a website. Well-designed content is like a skilled and pleasant solution vendor brought onto the website. It clarifies the customer's current situation and helps the customer solve her or his problem or fulfill her or his needs (Figure 5.3). The content also determines a large part of how reliable a company feels to a customer and how expert it seems. Without good content, it is impossible to make digital sales. We describe the textual content of the website in more detail in Section 5.2.1.

	What does the visitor do?		What a website needs to have		What will happen
R	Searches something from a search engine	>	Content and technic implementation are search engine optimized	>	Visitor comes to the website
A	Looks for something specific from the website	>	Website is clear and coherent and guides towards a goal	>	Visitor makes the desired action
C	Wants to contact you	>	Easily accessable and fillable contact form, contact information always easily available	>	Visitor makes a contact request
E	Visitor commits or subscribes to the service	>	Constantly updating content on the website and emails	>	Visitor engages / spends time with your brand

Figure 5.3   The website guides the customer towards a purchase when it adapts to the customer's needs

A well-functioning website generates leads and customers from website visitors, for example, in the following way. When a visitor searches for information on a search engine, he or she ends up on the website because it is well search engine optimized (i.e., easy to find). Once the visitor arrives at the website, he or she starts looking for the additional information he or she needs. With a consistent and clear website structure, the visitor is more likely to find what he or she is looking for and spend more time on the website. However, the time spent on the website does not directly translate into revenue, which is why the visitor must be able to contact the company easily and quickly in a number of ways, such as through clickable phone numbers, a chat feature, or forms in the footer.

LEGO provides an example of how to make shopping easier on a website. By visiting the LEGO website, you will get a good idea of how the target groups have been taken into account. When you reach the LEGO website, you will first encounter a banner from which you can click to choose to either play games or shop on LEGO's official website. Young children presumably choose to play games and watch videos. An adult, on the other hand, is more likely to choose to go to the shop so that he or she can shop or ask for support for the products.

BOX 5.1   WORDPRESS: A WEBSITE PUBLISHING PLATFORM

About a third of all websites on the Internet are already made with WordPress, making it the most widely used website platform in the world. With its high popularity, its open source is surrounded by a large number of people, keeping it constantly updated and keeping its features and security up to date. WordPress is easy to maintain, so anyone in your company can enter textual content, such as blog posts, on your company's website. WordPress does not tie a company to a single service provider or marketing partner as many people already use WordPress.

The visuals and functionality of WordPress pages are almost limitless, so you can make them look just the way you want them to look. Different add-ons allow you to add various required features to your website, such as counters or a chat add-on. WordPress pages are also search engine-friendly because they load quickly and it is easy to edit page titles and meta descriptions for search engines. In addition, the WooCommerce add-on makes it easy to connect your e-commerce site to your WordPress site.

Especially for larger website implementations with a budget of over €50,000, the Drupal publishing system has been used more than WordPress in the past. Today, WordPress is also increasingly used to build large websites, and for example, the redesign of the Finnish Road Safety Council website was implemented with WordPress.

CASE STUDY
CASE EXAMPLE: RENOVATION OF LEHTO'S WEBSITE

Lehto is a Finnish construction and real estate group whose motto is "a forerunner of a better tomorrow." Lehto's operations are driven by the desire to be ahead of its time and to renew the construction industry and thereby generate value, that is, a better tomorrow for its customers. In practice, it means high-quality, affordable, fast, and ecological construction.

Lehto sets the goals of its marketing as being to increase direct sales and increase brand awareness in the longer term. Without a clear marketing model, it would be impossible to systematically lead the marketing of such a large company towards set goals. That is why Lehto chose the MRACE® model to support the implementation of its marketing. The implementation of the MRACE® model began with the redesign of Lehto's website because the old website did not serve its goals properly. In connection with the website reform, digital customer paths for different buyer personas and a social media strategy were created and systematic campaigning was continued.

THE NEW WEBSITE IS A SOLUTION VENDOR ONLINE

The task of the solution vendor is to propose the most suitable solution for the customer's needs. Lehto's new website was built on the same principle. Its task was to help and guide Lehto's customers when the seller is not available or when the customer wants to search for information independently.

At the heart of the website reform were customer paths, whose importance is stressed in Lehto's industry sector. In the construction and real estate sector, it is typical that the information-search and evaluation phases are very long, leading to a situation where the purchasing process is interrupted many times before the actual decision is made. Clear customer paths make it easier for a customer to continue her or his purchasing process, search for information, and get to know the company, regardless of whether she or he has an active conversation with the company.

Thanks to the new website, Lehto took a big step towards even more digital sales. In many cases, a company website is the first meeting point between a customer and a company. Therefore, one should invest in its ease of use as it shapes the brand image in the desired direction.

5.2   CONTENT MARKETING

Content marketing is a very broad concept that everyone seems to interpretate differently. Basically, content marketing can mean everything a company does in terms of producing content, ranging from their PowerPoint presentations to social media posts and from giant blog articles of 10,000 words to a one-minute brand video. In this book, we focus on three themes of content marketing: the textual content written on a company's website, videos, and visual design.

Properly done content marketing affects every step of the MRACE® model. A company reaches more customers with search engine-optimized content (in the Reach phase), good content and logical buying paths make site visitors more likely to become leads (in the Act phase), landing pages that encourage selling and are impactful make the website visitor behave on the website in the manner that the company wants, for instance, the visitor requests an offer (in the Convert phase), and by using content that teaches customers how to use a product or service and by providing expert content, the customers become more engaged with the company (in the Engage stage).

5.2.1 A website's textual content

All digital marketing relies heavily on the content marketing on the website. As we have emphasized in this book, if the website's content marketing does not get the customer to act in the way the company wants, the entire marketing process is practically wasted. The company's reputation is growing, but it cannot be used to pay employees' salaries.

Let us take an example. Imagine there are two doors in front of you. You open the first door. Behind the door is a salesperson who starts presenting a product he is selling to you quickly and in a vague tone. He constantly fails to answer your questions, and the pushy attitude makes you feel uncomfortable. You move to the next door. The seller of this room starts by asking about your needs and the challenges you want to solve. You answer, and the seller tells you what results others with the same problem have had with his product. In addition, the seller can read the situation and answer your questions even before you have asked them. Would you not rather buy the product from the latter seller?

Most of the content on companies' websites represents one of these vendors. When a visitor arrives at a company's website, does he or she encounter a pushy salesperson or a solution-focused salesperson? The content of the website determines who wants to collaborate with the company, as well as how many are converted to sales leads and how much sales are generated.

5.2.1.1 Building a buying path to your website using buyer personas

It is important for a company to remember that all the content is created *for* its customers. That is why it is important to know what things a company's buyer personas want more information on and what things they need help with. When doing content marketing, the most important thing is to find out the factor that drives the purchase decisions of the buyers most (i.e., the driver). Once the driver for a buyer persona is known, it should be highlighted in the content intended for that buyer persona. In this case, the buyer persona begins to want more value offered by the product or service and is not just looking for the lowest price on the market. Customers who buy a product because of the value it produces are also much more likely to commit to the company selling the product.

Once the company's buyer personas have been identified, separate purchase paths are built for them, based on the driver guiding each buyer persona. The goal is to guide the customer from being an information seeker to being a committed customer. Purchasing paths are best built when the driver that guides the buyer persona is kept at the center of all the content on the buying path. The company must therefore systematically make use of the buyer persona's driver and turn it into willingness to buy the product offered by the company. In this way, a company does not gather one-time buyers but customers who want to buy a product or service because of the value it produces.

Take an example where one person wants to save on heating costs in his or her home and another person wants to reduce her or his carbon footprint. The needs of these two buyer personas are completely different, but a geothermal heat pump, for example, can be one solution for both needs. Due to the different drivers, two purchase paths have to be built in this case, so that the need of both buyer personas is channeled into the desire to buy a geothermal pump.

Content marketing that is based on drivers also develops the brand. When the driver guiding the buyer persona is also present in the content of the website, the customer compares her or his user experience to the promise made on the website. If the product meets her or his expectations, the experience is often powerful. In this case, the image of the company in the customer's mind develops in accordance with the value of the product and the customer's experience. The company's brand also develops based on the kind of customer base the company manages to attract. Many customers wonder what kind of people prefer certain kinds of product or service, or a certain brand. When a company gathers the desired customer base through content marketing, its brand develops in exactly the desired direction.

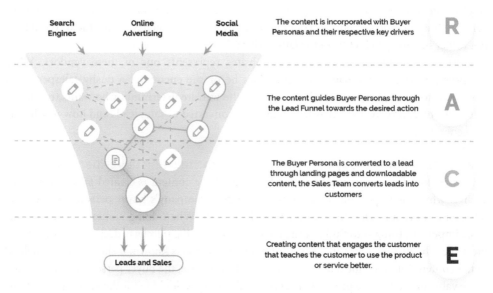

The content is incorporated with Buyer Personas and their respective key drivers — **R**

The content guides Buyer Personas through the Lead Funnel towards the desired action — **A**

The Buyer Persona is converted to a lead through landing pages and downloadable content, the Sales Team converts leads into customers — **C**

Creating content that engages the customer that teaches the customer to use the product or service better. — **E**

Figure 5.4   Through purchase paths, website visitors become leads no matter how they have arrived at the website

Carefully constructed buying paths generate leads from website visitors no matter how they enter the site (Fiigure 5.4). Purchasing paths are built on the website so that all the content intended for a specific buyer persona is linked. It is also important that each content item creates the desire and interest to read the next content item, otherwise the customer will not move on to the next content item and the purchase path will stop.

Let us take an imaginary example of what a buying path might be in practice. A customer searches for information online by typing "How to save on heating costs in a detached house" in the search box of a search engine. She ends up at a blog that discusses five different ways to save on heating costs. Readers of the blog are segmented by links to slightly more specific content so that they are directed to the next, slightly more specific content item by links. For example, the resident of an electrically heated house is directed to the content "How do you save on the heating costs of an electrically heated house?" from which she is led to the next, more detailed content item "How much does a geothermal pump save on the cost of electric heating? Read five examples." The content on the geothermal heat pump already provides the customer with a product selection guide entitled "Choose the correct geothermal heat pump to maximize energy savings: Five criteria for purchasing a geothermal heat pump." The customer stays on the website for half an hour and ends up buying a geothermal heat pump.

Properly made buying paths are of great importance to the functioning of marketing in its entirety. The previous two examples were, of course, rough simplifications of purchasing paths, and especially in the B2B industries the purchasing paths are often much more complex as numerous people are involved in decision-making who all look at it from different perspectives. In B2C industries, too, the acquisition of more valuable products can easily be considered for years. However, it does not remove the importance of the buying path, on the contrary, it increases it.

5.2.1.2   Channels bring visitors, the website generates leads

Currently, paid advertising is becoming more common, which is why the importance of content marketing is further emphasized (Figure 5.5). The more competition there is in paid advertising channels, the more expensive paid advertising will become. Within a few years, we will probably be in a situation where poorly converted pages are simply not worth promoting in a competitive industry until the website generates leads with the desired conversion rate. In the US, for example, advertising on digital channels is already significantly more expensive than in Finland.

Let us take an example of how website development improves the cost-effectiveness of advertising. Imagine that Google and Facebook drive a total of 6,000 visitors to your site each month. If your site has a conversion rate of 1 percent, you will generate 60 leads per month. To double the number of leads, you can either try to double the number of visitors to 12,000 per month or improve your website's conversion rate from 1 percent to 2 percent with content marketing. Developing a conversion rate is always a more sustainable and affordable choice, and one of the best ways to do that is through content marketing.

The result of content marketing scales strongly over time as new content is always built on top of previous content (Figure 5.6). This creates a certain kind of compound interest rate effect. Let us think that the same amount of resources are used for content each month, be the resources time or money. The content produced in previous months will yield results each month after it is produced. The content can also be imagined here as sellers: If there is one seller in the first company and 100 sellers in the second, which company will make more sales assuming the sellers are equally good?

Another thing worth noting is that if content marketing is done in a search engine-optimized way, its impact will go a long way. Thus, if content marketing is done for ten years and is suddenly stopped, the content marketing that has already been done will generate revenue for several more years. If, on the other hand, paid advertising is carried out for ten years and is suddenly stopped, no more revenue will be gained from the paid advertising. Of course,

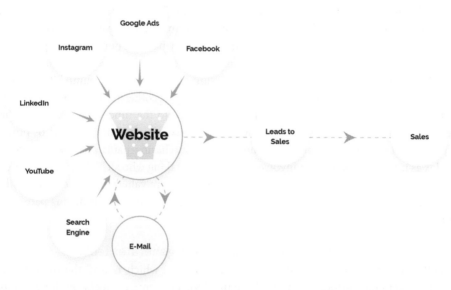

Figure 5.5   All digital marketing eventually directs the potential customer to the company's website; creating a website that is as sellable and easy to use as possible is the best way to improve the cost-effectiveness of your advertising

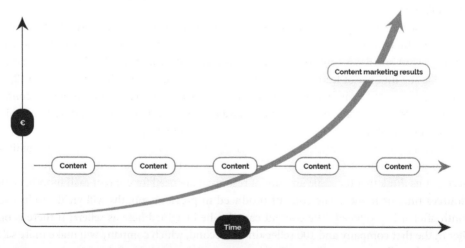

Figure 5.6   Scaling the results of content marketing

this does not mean that paid advertising should be stopped and that all resources should be devoted to content creation; properly done paid advertising is very profitable, and in many industries, it is a lifeline. The example illustrates how long-term results are generated by content marketing and how its nature differs from that of paid advertising.

There is confusion about content marketing when it is just seen as writing that anyone who is literate can do. It is true that anyone can write content, but very few can write it in a way that produces results. In other words, anyone can write a text about the benefits of jogging. Very few can write it so that the reader goes for a run after reading the text.

We live amid such a huge flood of messages that we do not want to read a text or watch a video if we do not find it useful or entertaining. Therefore, buyer personas need to be created accurately as this is the only way to build interesting content around customers' problems and needs. When the content speaks to the customer and focuses on solving his or her problems, the customer will read the content for anything up to several hours if necessary.

5.2.2 Videos

Most buying decisions are fundamentally driven by emotions. Without emotion, there would be no temptation to buy. A video tells the story of a service or product precisely in a form that evokes emotion. It can nail a customer's attention, entice her or him to visit a website, and teach her or him how a product or service works. With a video, a company can give a flying start to a new product launch or rebrand an old product. A video is also a powerful tool for recruiting new employees as it attracts the attention of potential employees with proven effectiveness. A video can also provide a peephole to the company's culture and introduce the company and its staff, promoting the image of the employer.

5.2.2.1 The production of marketing videos

The production process for marketing videos involves four main stages: production planning, video filming, post-production, and feedback and follow-up (Figure 5.7).

- *Production planning*: The production plan explains why the video is being made, what or who is being filmed, and where and when the video is being filmed. Setting a goal is the most important step in a production plan. The goal of the video should go hand in hand with buyer personas and the different stages of their path to purchase. The target audience is defined through the identification of buyer personas. Publishing channels are also directly related to the buyer personas. Ask yourself in which channels customers can be reached with video. Based on the publishing channels, it is known how long the videos can be in the first place, in what aspect ratio the video must be produced, and the available advertising options. Instagram, Facebook, YouTube, and other channels have their own rules that define video production from a technical standpoint.

    Only after setting a goal is it decided what will be filmed, where, and when. In addition, when designing a video, it is important to consider your target audiences and publishing channels in order to identify a suitable video genre, ambience, and highlights.

    When designing videos, you also need to know the marketing strategy because the videos are designed entirely with the company's other marketing efforts in mind. The call to action for the video must be clear and in line with other marketing activities. A call to action could be, for example, "Read more on our website and request a quote." Of course, a lot of videos are also produced for other use cases, such as various brand videos, educational videos, and employer branding videos. Even then, it is helpful to know if your video is intended to be used for paid advertising.

At the end of the production planning, the videos are scripted, the project is scheduled, the background music for the video is selected, and the audio clips are recorded.

- *Video filming*: Usually, filming days include filming several interviews and events. The aim is to make the stored material match the predefined plan as closely as possible. Filming is the only step in the video production process that usually requires simultaneous physical presence and schedules from videographers and customers.
- *Post-production*: After the video material is filmed, its post-production begins. Post-production involves all the activities related to the processing of video material: video cutting, color definition, sound design, special effects, subtitles, etc. This is the most arduous step for videographers. Once a draft of the video is complete, the customer will review and comment on the video, after which the necessary tweaks and changes will be made. The end result is a finished video production.
- *Feedback and follow-up*: About a month after the video production was completed, it is good to go through how well the results met the set goals and what was learned from all this.

Figure 5.7   Things to consider in the production of marketing videos

5.2.2.2   Videos in the different stages of the MRACE® model

The different stages of the MRACE® model require different styles of video because the buyers are at different stages in the buying process. Slightly longer and slower-paced videos are suitable for the Act and Convert stages, but do not work for the Reach stage. In contrast, the fast and short videos typical of the Reach phase do not add any value to the buyer in the Act phase.

In the Reach stage, the only function of a video is to nail down the viewer's attention and get them to click on the ad link. The optimal duration for a Reach-stage video is 5–30 seconds. Since there is only a negligible time window in which to convince the viewer, the video needs to go straight to the point. So, you especially have to focus on the first seconds of the video; the viewer's attention needs to be nailed down visually as (on most channels) the video starts without sound by default. If there is speech in the video, it is necessary that the video is also clearly subtitled.

In the Act stage, the most important function of a video is to engage the viewer with a service, product, or brand. The optimal duration for an Act-stage video is 1–5 minutes. An Act-stage video is often embedded in landing pages or in paid advertising. On the landing page, the performance of a video can be measured, for example, via downloads of a specific publication (a guide, whitepaper, digital magazine), as a result of which, the viewer becomes a lead. In advertising, the percentage of video consumption by viewers can be used as a measure of video performance. On Facebook, for example, follow-up action can be targeted directly at an audience that has viewed a specific percentage of the video (e.g., at least 50 percent). An audience that has watched a long video at least halfway is likely to be interested in the product, service, or brand and thus may represent a potential customer.

In the Convert phase, the main function of a video is to convert the viewer into a customer. What is essential in the video is that the call to action is clearly visible to the viewer. A Convert video can be used on a landing page or in advertising. The content of such a video depends on what type of product is being marketed in the video. When marketing a simple consumer product to the general public, such as toothpaste or a soft drink, the video should be short and concise, lasting about 10 to 30 seconds. When selling a specialty product to an enlightened audience, such as a camera backpack, an air-source heat pump, or educational course, the video must have enough substance to convince the audience. This inevitably also means a longer video.

An Engage-stage video promotes customer retention by teaching the customer to use the product or service better. It can also produce additional sales by providing an existing customer with information about a new product. In addition, videos that guide you through the use of a product or service serve as content marketing for new customers. Engage-stage videos can be used on a website or blog and in email marketing, advertising, or the company's customer portal.

A video is a great way to remind a customer about a product, service, brand, or job vacancy. The role of remarketing is to grab the viewer's attention, remind them of the offer, get them to click on the ad, and return them to the landing page where conversion can take place. In general, remarketing should favor short, 15–30-second videos as the viewer is already familiar with the offer (the viewer has either visited the company's website before or watched a certain amount of some previous video).

It is also possible to build video series on Facebook and YouTube. Video ads can be triggered so that when a viewer watches a certain percentage of the ad, they will be shown a new video next time. The customer can thus be guided along the purchase path one video at a time.

From the same video material, it is possible to produce both longer and shorter videos for different stages of the purchase path. This saves time and production costs compared with producing videos for each stage separately. We recommend a minimum of three videos for each marketing and recruitment campaign:

1. A Reach-stage video that brings visitors to the landing page.
2. An Act-/Convert-stage video that tells the visitor on the landing page more about the offering.
3. A remarketing video that returns interested visitors back to the landing page.

Diversifying video content can also be used for testing different sales arguments. For example, a long video of more than a minute in the Act or Convert stage often includes three to five different selling points. Each of these can be cut down to a short 5–30-second video ad that can be used in the Reach stage. By A/B testing the ads (i.e., by comparing the performance of two different ads) you can get an idea of which arguments will best resonate with your target audience and what angles your videos and other marketing activities should adopt in the future.

5.2.3   Visual design

The visual look of a company determines what kind of first impression the company gives to its customers. A first impression can only be given once, which is why it is important that the customer's thoughts on the brand are heading in the right direction from the very beginning. In addition, a unified visual look strengthens the brand and increases its recognizability in various channels and media. The purpose of visual design is to support and clarify communication through colors, layout, fonts, photographs, and other graphics. On the website, it enhances the customer's user experience and guides his or her actions as desired.

Most purchase decisions are made when the buyer's perception of the product matches the buyer's desired perception. Creating the right kind of image is important because it makes the customer engage with the brand longer, in addition to making the brand promise stronger. For example, what is the image of a cleaning company with a dark brown and blurry website compared with one with light and fresh pages? Because brown, murkiness and ambiguity signal dirt and clutter, the latter company is likely to create a better image for the customer. In reality, companies can be very equal in terms of competence, but their visual image may differ greatly. It is very common for the visual appearance to create a worse image of the company than actually is the case. The visual design therefore plays a crucial role in how the customer perceives the competence of the company.

A unified visual design can also help a company to engage the buyers as its regular customers. By maintaining a unified visual look, the company helps the customer recognize the company in all channels, from social media to the company's website. Recognizability is one of the most important indicators of brand value. For example, if you are buying new sports shoes, you will probably pay more attention to shoes that are offered by the brands that you recognize as most people are more likely to buy from a company they are familiar with and recognize.

The more often a customer comes across the brand look of a particular company, the better it stays in the customer's mind and the more familiar it begins to feel. A feeling of familiarity, in turn, is key to building trust, which in turn is a prerequisite for trading. A unified look across all channels is therefore the easiest and also the most effective way to increase the customer's impression that a company is familiar and reliable. With a unified look, the entire brand's look is also more manageable (Figure 5.8).

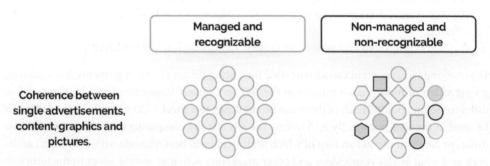

Figure 5.8   With a unified look, a company creates recognizability

A visual look can also be used to communicate a company's values to a target audience as a person whose values match the company's values is more likely to end up as a paying customer. By the combination of appealing visuals and content, values are made visible, which engages customers in the company and promotes customer acquisition. If, for example, one of the company's values is environmental friendliness, a mere green leaf near some text reinforces the message.

The customers of competing companies are often very similar to each other. Therefore, the visual appearances of companies in the same industry may also resemble each other. When designing a visual look, it is important to adopt the predominant look of the industry, yet clearly different from your competitors. One good way to do this is to highlight the company's values in the visuals because they allow the company to develop its brand and appeal to the target group it wants.

If the look of the company is similar to that of its competitors, the company will appear to be equal to everyone else in the eyes of the customer. When a company stands out, it gets more attention and becomes a more identifiable player. When designing a visual look, other players in the industry need to be thoroughly analyzed: What is the look of the competitors? And How can you build a recognizable look that stands out from theirs?

5.2.3.1   Visual design as part of the MRACE® model

Visual design is connected to and affects every step of the MRACE® model.

- *Reach*: A company that strongly stands out visually from its competitors immediately gets a competitive advantage. Even if the customer does not yet know the company, the likelihood of a purchase increases when the advertising and website grab the customer's attention and look trustworthy.
- *Act*: Visual design makes it possible to build a priority order between the elements of a website. By talking about creating a *priority order*, we refer to visually emphasizing the elements to which the visitor should pay attention. Such highlights guide the customer forward on the purchase path.
- *Convert*: The buying experience is made user-friendly and easy to understand by clearly highlighting all the things that facilitate purchasing. This will remove barriers to purchasing and generate interest, even when the customer is simply browsing the site quickly.
- *Engage*: From the very first stage, customers have built a strong image of what the company looks like. Once the image of the company's visual look is fixed in the customer's mind and she or he comes across the company's ad later, she or he recognizes the company.
- *Measure*: A visual look can be considered successful when it creates the desired image of the company for customers. Success or failure is tested with surveys that find out customers' opinions about the company's visual look. Alternatively, the customer may be asked to list, for example, seven adjectives that he or she believes best reflect the look and feel of the company. A/B testing can be used to find out which style of ad works best on Facebook, for example, in terms of its visual appearance.

CASE STUDY
CASE EXAMPLE: THE POWER OF SIPARILA'S MULTI-CHANNEL CONTENT MARKETING

Siparila offers the most comprehensive range of wood construction products in Finland. The range consists of interior, exterior, and sauna panels, as well as yard construction products. The company's main target groups are all people working in wood construction, from consumers and architects to large nationwide timber and construction stores.

INCREASING PRODUCT AND BRAND AWARENESS IS AT THE HEART OF MARKETING

Siparila has been in business for a long time, but their challenge in marketing was very typical: excellent products had not been communicated in a memorable way. Therefore, the most important goals of marketing were to increase product and brand awareness. With the help of these two goals, demand was increased in all target groups both via Siparila's channels and its reseller network.

Due to the wide range of products, it was initially decided that marketing should focus on certain top products. The landing pages of these products were carefully finalized—both visually and in terms of content (the Convert stage)—and various blog posts (in the Reach, Act, Engage stages) were built around the products for different buyer personas. With these activities, demand for the products increased and resellers learned to sell Siparila's products better to consumers. The leverage that content brings to sales thus extends to the sales speeches of the resellers.

A major role in raising the awareness of the company was to create a thought leader position by taking a stand on the major themes surrounding wood construction. Making values visible in marketing and in a firm's operations makes any business more approachable and interesting. In this way, the company is able to strengthen its position as an industry expert, which increases the customer's interest (in the Convert stage) and commitment (in the Engage stage) to the company.

HOW WAS THE CONTENT DISTRIBUTED TO BUYERS?

Siparila's products are both beautiful and highly technical. Thus, communication could be designed in a variety of content formats using images, videos, and informative text. The Reach stage was designed so that Instagram acted as a source of inspiration and as a community builder, Facebook was deployed for results-based advertising in order to reach new interested audiences, and Google Ads and SEO were used to respond to customers' product and problem queries.

When the product range is wide, not everything can be fixed right away. Therefore, Siparila's approach to marketing was a wise choice from a strategic point of view; concentrating on one product group at a time will get its marketing off to a good start, after which supportive activities are enough to maintain a good performance level.

A FEW KEY FIGURES

REACH

The amount of organic site traffic increased by 74 percent compared with the previous year.

Social media reached 297 percent more people (700,000) than in the previous year, although the budget was only increased by 98 percent.

ACT

The total number of site visitors increased by 181 percent compared with the previous year.

The number of product page views increased by 42 percent compared with the previous year.

CONVERT

As many as 418 requests for quotations were received in half a year, which is almost twice as many as before.

The number of people who went to reseller pages through Google increased by 57 percent.

ENGAGE

There were 22,129 returning visitors to the site during the first half of the year, which means that the site engages visitors well.

5.3 SEARCH ENGINE MARKETING AND ONLINE ADVERTISING

Search engine marketing (SEM) is the marketing of a website or service on search engines. The search engine in the Finnish market is almost always Google as it is by far the most used search engine in Finland. Other search engines include Yahoo, Yandex, Bing, Baidu, and DuckDuckGo. Due to Google's overwhelming popularity, we will only focus on Google in this book when it comes to SEM.

SEM involves two major marketing techniques: SEO and SEA. After that, we will cover Google's core online advertising services including the Google Display Network, Google Discovery Ads, and YouTube advertising.

We are probably right to claim that you use Google to search for information when you make an informed purchasing decision. Let that be a good justification for the importance of SEM because we can guarantee that if you are, you are not the only one doing so.

5.3.1   Search engine optimization (SEO)

SEO improves and increases the amount and quality of organic traffic to a website by improving the search engine visibility of the site. SEO is not a quick action as search engines take numerous factors into account when determining search rankings, in addition to which, competition for free or organic visibility is constantly increasing. Still, SEO is considered the cornerstone of digital marketing because the more organic traffic a website has, the more digital marketing is on stable ground. If a company's marketing relies entirely on paid advertising and the money taps suddenly have to close (as happened in the spring of 2020 due to COVID-19), marketing will stop completely. Good organic search visibility is not affected by global crises.

SEO has traditionally meant technical SEO as well as the creation of search engine-optimized content. Today, Google values more and more sites that are easy to use and have a great user experience. Therefore, SEO now needs to be accompanied by a third component, conversion rate optimization (CRO) (note that the term conversion optimization is also used). The better user experience created by CRO is likely to be further emphasized in the future as the amount of content is predicted to explode with content written by AI. If anyone can write a 5,000-word blog post in minutes with the help of AI in the near future, Google will have to change its search-ranking algorithm, even radically. It is exciting to see how AI content is going to transform SEO and digital marketing overall.

The main goal of SEO is to increase the traffic to a website. Getting organic traffic to your website is, of course, important, but getting your visitor to behave in the way you want on your site (e.g., getting her or him to download a guide or request a quote) is more important. Therefore, SEO needs to be linked to buyer personas and buying paths. With CRO, traffic to your site is finally taken advantage of with a better user experience, turning as many visitors as possible into paying customers.

When SEO, CRO, and quality content production are combined, a website achieves its full conversion potential. The ability of a website to generate leads and trade is one of the most critical stages of digital marketing because all marketing ultimately leads to a website. For example, if you get a recommendation from a friend about a company while jogging together, that too will often lead you to that company's website in the end. Therefore, how well a website directs site visitors towards requesting a quote, purchasing a product, or getting in touch affects the overall outcome of your marketing, regardless of how the visitor came to your site.

5.3.1.1   Improving search rankings

The first goal of SEO is to make your site perform better and rise in Google search results. This occurs in the Reach phase of the MRACE® model. The following are three things you need to do to get a better position in the search results (Figure 5.9):

1. Create content based on keyword research.
2. Have a website with first-class technical functionality.
3. Have a strong domain.

If you want to increase your search ranking, these three areas must also be continuously developed. Otherwise, rankings in the search engines will not rise, they will fall.

- *Content based on keyword research*: Keyword research finds out what terms customers use to search for a company's products. The better the content of your site matches your customers' searches, the more traffic your website receives. However, a high search ranking alone does not mean that visitors will turn into business as website traffic alone will not put a single euro in the cashbox. Therefore, in the strategy phase, buyer personas are created so that the content can be built around the buyer personas' purchasing processes. In this case, the content systematically directs visitors to, for example, request a quote or download a guide.

  High search rankings can be compared to a brick-and-mortar store: how high a website appears in the search results corresponds to how well a brick-and-mortar store is located. However, the central location of a brick-and-mortar store does not guarantee that customers will buy anything. Therefore, the store needs to be made consistent and all barriers to buying need to be removed; on a website, this means creating buying paths with content and CRO of the site.

- *The first-class technical functionality of the website*: By *technical functionality*, we mean that the website works properly for both the user and Google. Under the hood of a website, there are hundreds of small factors that affect search rankings. Even the slightest mistake can prevent Google's crawler from accessing your website, meaning that your entire website will not be able to appear in search results at all. When a website is technically working properly, it also becomes much faster, which has a positive effect on search rankings and the customer experience.

- *A strong domain*: If the domain is strong, search engines will see it as trusted and popular. So, the stronger the domain, the more likely Google is to promote your website. A strong domain is most affected by how many other websites link to that website as the links appear to Google's search algorithms as recommendations for that website. When other websites want to link to your website, it makes your website trustworthy in the eyes of Google. Who would want to link to a bad website from their own website?

Such links can be acquired both actively and passively. *Active link acquisition* means, among other things, that if a company is mentioned on a website, the company contacts the website and asks the website to add a link to the company's website. *Passive link acquisition* is done through quality content. When high-quality content is produced for a website, those who write about similar topics can, if they wish, create a link to the website to add value to their readers.

SEO should be developed by first analyzing the data collected from the website in order to make a plan and hypotheses. For example, a company may find that key blog posts on its website have not risen in Google's search results. Based on this, a plan is made in which the links to these blog posts are added to the footer of the site. The plan is put into practice, after which its success can be accurately measured. After a month, the company notices that these blog posts have started to rise in Google's search results, so they decide to apply the same tactics to a few other blog posts. When the results of SEO are constantly monitored, as in the previous example, and based on the results, hypotheses and plans are created, development

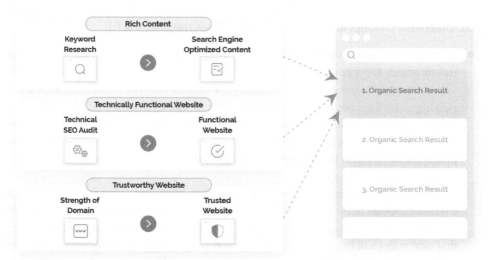

Figure 5.9   The three most important areas of SEO are keyword-based content, first-class technical functionality, and a strong domain name

becomes an ongoing part of marketing. Continuous improvement allows you to find the best SEO techniques for your site as quickly as possible.

5.3.1.2   Conversion rate optimization (CRO)

CRO in this context means improving the salability and ease of use of a website with the help of information gathered through various tools. In practice, this means that the website is constantly evolving to better meet customer needs, making customers find what they are looking for faster and making asking for a quote or buying a product more likely. If your business website receives a lot of visitors but no purchases, leads, or contacts, CRO tells you where to find the problem. CRO supports digital sales because it makes it easier for the customer to progress along the purchase path by removing barriers to purchase. Developing your website to be more customer-friendly through CRO is extremely important as even very small changes can make a big difference in regard to achieving a more positive customer experience.

CRO also has a significant impact on SEO. The longer visitors spend on a website and the more pages they browse, the better Google interprets that website. In that case, Google is more likely to rank that website higher in search results because it wants to direct its customers to the best possible websites.

Conversion means achieving a measurable goal, such as sending a form, buying a product from an online store, or joining an email list. The *conversion rate*, on the other hand, refers to the percentage of visitors to your website who act as desired and accomplish one of your conversion goals. However, a website's overall conversion rate is usually a pretty poor metric that does not say much. For example, an ongoing recruitment campaign may completely confuse a website's overall conversion rate. Sure, that metric gives an indication of how well a website engages visitors and how well paid advertising has succeeded in getting the right kind of visitors to your website, but it does not tell you anything very specific or concrete.

CRO should always start with strategy work because hundreds of website details can be filed better, but in reality, only a handful of changes are important for the end result. The strategy is used to collect data about users in order to be able to really improve the business-relevant sections of the website.

As part of your CRO strategy, you will find out what your website's worst pain points are and how you can improve the customer experience. To this end, the website should be audited in order to gather quantitative and qualitative information about the activities of website visitors. The result is a comprehensive plan with which to solve challenges related to the usability of the website, content, and technical functionality. Before you begin CRO, you should answer at least the following questions: Where are we now? What problems need to be solved? What is needed to solve the problems? What are the obstacles to the proposed solutions? Once these questions have been answered, CRO will be easier to implement.

The data collection process for CRO (Figure 5.10) begins with an analysis of the data collected from the website and, based on the analysis, the development targets for the website are found, which will be achieved by testing various remedies for the website; finally, the effects of the actions are measured and analyzed.

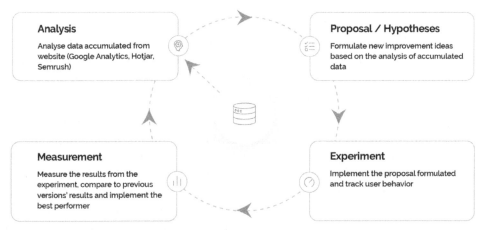

Figure 5.10   The data collection process for CRO

In a quantitative study, a website is initially covered by a comprehensive technical review that identifies the website's problem areas: Does the website work properly with all devices and their different browsers? Does the website have technical issues that cause website users headaches or even prevent conversions? Are there any challenges to website speed—especially during mobile usage—that should be addressed? Following the technical review, user activity is mapped using a survey of Google Analytics to determine the stages of a customer's purchase path and their conversion rates. In addition, the bounce rate of the main landing pages from different traffic sources is examined to see if, for example, traffic from social media has a higher bounce rate than traffic from Google. If the difference is significant in favor of one source of traffic over another, it is worth considering how the less well-functioning source of traffic could be improved.

Qualitative research examines the reasons behind users' actions: What do users think when they see a product? What do users want? Why are users on the website? What do users do on the website? Information is collected from other contact channels, such as chat logs, contact forms, and customer surveys.

Website changes should not be made at will, they should be done with CRO tools. The tools can be used to track the behavior of visitors to a website. Valuable information to collect includes information on what your visitors are doing on the website, the most popular landing pages, and the biggest pain points on your website that are preventing a conversion from taking place. One of the key tools for website analysis is Hotjar.

Useful features of the tools include the following:

- *Heatmaps*: Heatmaps visually show which points users click on and where on the website they lose interest in the content and stop browsing. If most visitors stop reading a text in the middle of it but one of the most important things in the text comes at the end, the structure of the text needs to be changed.
- *Recordings of visitor movements on the website*: The recordings concretely show how the visitor navigates the website and whether he or she gets stuck somewhere in the buying process due to a poorly designed buying path.
- *Form analysis*: This feature reveals how users enter information into forms and whether there are sections in the forms that can be developed to increase the form-fill rate.
- *Page-specific queries*: The surveys ask the customer directly about the pain points, about what could be better on the website, and about whether they found what they needed. This simple measure often results in excellent development proposals.

Based on the information gathered, it is advisable to prioritize issues that require action. At the same time, development suggestions are created to solve the problems: Is this a usability problem? Is the information provided by the website unclear? Is the solution provided by the website useful to the user? Is there a technical issue with this website? Sometimes even very small changes result in a percentage increase in conversions. Sometimes the solution may require significantly more work, such as a complete overhaul of the product page or a redesign of the top navigation of the entire site. If possible, development suggestions should be reviewed with a larger team so that in addition to the information gathered, different perspectives on the situation are obtained.

Figure 5.11 shows what CRO can accomplish, for example, for an online store. Based on the analysis, the following problem is found: products are added to the cart, but there are few purchases. Hotjar recordings show that some products are not stored in the shopping cart, which impairs the usability of the store. When the problem is fixed, the conversion rate increases from 1.5 percent to 2.6 percent.

It is important to understand that if no improvements are made, it will put a brake on all marketing. The website is at the heart of all digital marketing, and traffic from other marketing channels—such as television, radio, and print media—also comes to the website. If a website does not work the way your company wants it to, a large portion of the sales potential it generates is wasted.

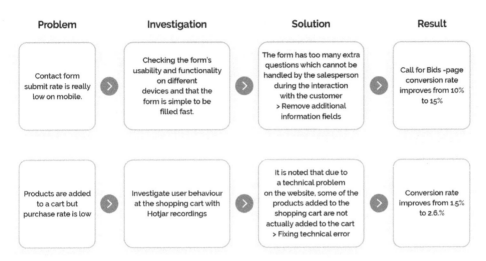

Figure 5.11   A practical example of what CRO can accomplish

Websites need to be continuously improved based on data and changes in customers' purchasing behavior. Customers are rapidly embracing new technologies that they can leverage in their purchasing process. For example, a few years ago, chatbots seemed strange to many, but at the moment, companies that do not take advantage of chatbots are likely to lose business. You should feel free to try new tools and channels to find out if they are suitable for marketing your business.

The purpose of continuous CRO is for the company to constantly test something new and thus be among the first to find the best ways to increase the result generated by marketing (Figure 5.12). In continuous CRO, hypotheses are first made about how a bottleneck noticed in the buying path could be avoided. The hypotheses are then tested in collaboration with the website developers and their effects are measured. A report is then made on the change, and it is reflected in how the company acts in similar situations in the future. After this, the process is started again from the beginning. In this way, the customers' purchasing path is constantly improving and as many of the website visitors as possible become paying customers.

5.3.2   Search engine advertising (SEA)

SEA is advertising on search engines where the ad shown to a user is determined by the keyword and location used by the user. SEA ads appear at the top of a search engine's search results page. In SEA, an advertiser pays a certain amount to the search engine each time someone clicks on the ad's business page. The amount varies a lot depending on the region, keyword, season, and industry. As we said earlier, in this book we only deal with the most-used search engine in Finland, Google.

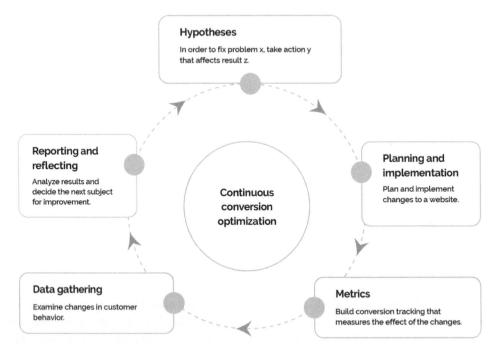

Figure 5.12 The process of continuous CRO

5.3.2.1 Google Ads SEA

Google Ads SEA is one of the most effective and measurable forms of marketing. A potential customer can become a paying customer very quickly if a visitor is directed directly from the ad to the correct landing page.

When planning your advertising, you need to carefully analyze what kind of pages a visitor is directed to and from which ad. If the right landing page is missing, it is a good idea to build it in order to improve your advertising performance. Naturally, the ads must be such that they attract clicks to the company's pages from a number of competing ads.

Advertising on the search network brings a lot of opportunities for a skilled actor as small margins in advertising make a big difference in the end result. For example, if the landing page that your ad directs visitors to converts better than a competitor's page, the company may pay more per click than the competitor. When you pay more for a click, your ad will appear higher on Google's search page, prompting potential customers to click on your company's website and click more rarely on a competitor's site.

The price of advertising is also affected by Google's quality score for advertising. The quality score is improved by improving your advertising, for example, through more accurate targeting and through better and more informative landing pages. The better your quality score, the less one click costs and the more likely your business is to reach the top of the Google search page, resulting in better advertising results.

The cost-effectiveness of advertising is largely determined by the keywords that trigger the ad. However, just as important for the cost-effectiveness of advertising is which keywords do not result in customers seeing your ads. Such keywords are called *negative keywords* and are used to avoid unnecessary clicks that would be unnecessarily costly. For example, if a car dealer does not add the word "toy" as a negative keyword, those looking for toy cars may end up on the car dealer's website. On the other hand, just "car" is a fairly vague search term, and not many people thinking about buying a car start their search process with the word "car." So when thinking about keywords, you need to step into the customer's boots and carefully consider the different scenarios that can be referred to by a particular keyword.

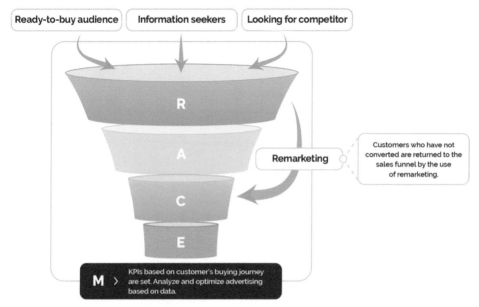

Figure 5.13 SEA can be done for both the Reach and Convert phases

The purpose of SEA is to direct the company's website to read-ready audiences, information seekers, and audiences seeking competitors. SEA is most effective when the customer is in the selection and evaluation phase. In this case, the customer is ready to buy but still compares the service providers before making a purchase decision. In contrast, Google Ads advertising makes it very difficult to reach customers who have not yet begun their purchase process. In such a situation it is better to advertise on YouTube, Discovery, Display, and social media advertising.

If a customer is directed to the website through advertising while their purchase process is in the selection and evaluation phase, the purchase decision may still be interrupted for one reason or another. In this case, as the service is already familiar to them from a previous website visit, the customer will be redirected directly from the Reach phase to the content of the Convert phase in order to request a quote, make a purchase, or download a guide (Figure 5.13).

Let us take an example of how the use of search terms tells you how close a customer is to making a purchase decision. When a customer uses the search term "loan" on Google, they know they need a loan but do not yet know what type of loan and where to get it. With such a general search term, search volumes are plentiful, but making a purchase decision still has many twists and turns. Your website should be very well conversion optimized so that you can even advertise to customers using such a very general search term. When a customer uses the search term "mortgage," he or she already knows what loan he or she needs but does not yet know from which bank to get it. For such a slightly more detailed search, where the customer is still in the evaluation stage, an extremely good landing page should be created that justifies why it is worth taking a mortgage from a particular bank. When a person uses the search term "mortgage + [the name of that bank]," the applicant has already defined exactly what he or she

Problem

Company has a solution to customer's problem, but the customer is not yet aware of it.

Information search

Company has a solution to customer's problem. Customer is aware of the alternatives to the solution, but searches for more information.

Selection/comparison

Company has a solution to customer's problem and customer is comparing various alternatives by different service providers.

Decision

Company has a solution to customer's problem and customer is ready to make the purchase decision.

> The closer the customer is to make a decision, the more it makes sense to pay for advertising, because the conversion is more likely to occur, leading to a probable deal in the near future.

Figure 5.14   The closer the customer is to making a purchase decision, the better the advertising result

wants and where he or she wants to get it. The buying potential is high if the website manages to quickly direct the applicant towards making contact, for example, requesting a loan offer.

So, it is a good idea to start with SEM by targeting audiences that are as close as possible to purchase because they are most likely to bring in quick sales (Figure 5.14). Therefore, it is also worth paying more for such audiences. Once advertising is effective for an audience close to making a purchase decision, it is a good idea to start scaling your advertising to an ever-widening and colder audience as long as it is clearly profitable for the advertiser. The role of measurement and data integrity in the scaling of advertising is emphasized. However, gaining transactions from a cold audience (consisting of people who have not yet shown interest in a company's products, but whose online activities show that they are potential customers for the company) often also requires developing a website so that its content creates buying paths that are specific to certain buyer personas.

5.3.3 Online advertising with Google's services

Online advertising means all paid advertising that utilizes the Internet. In this book, we will only cover Google's online advertising services under *online advertising*. Google's online advertising services are listed below:

- The Google Display Network
- Google Discovery Ads
- YouTube advertising
- Google Shopping.

Each of these four services is at its best when used in the Reach phase to reach new customers, but each can also be used in the Convert phase as a means of remarketing. However, we will not go into more detail about Google Shopping in this book as this channel is practically only suitable for the marketing of online stores.

5.3.3.1 Google Display advertising

The Google Display Network is the world's most comprehensive ad display network, reaching more than 90 percent of Internet users. The Google Display Network has evolved tremendously in recent years, especially in terms of identifying people and targeting advertising as Google provides more tools for identifying audiences. It allows advertising to be designed to reach different buyer personas. The Google Display Network's CPCs are also affordable compared with the Google search network, making it a cost-effective advertising channel when used properly.

Google Display Network ads can appear on a variety of websites, video content, and mobile applications. A display ad can be in the form of a text, image banner, or video ad. Almost all the banner ads you see online are Display Ads; you can look at them a little more closely next time and think about what the advertiser is trying to accomplish with that particular ad.

Google Display advertising is based on two components:

1. Directing potential, but cold, audiences to the website.
2. Returning warm audiences to your website through remarketing (Figure 5.15).

As previously noted, *cold audiences* consist of people who have not yet shown interest in a company's products, but whose online activities show that they are potential customers for the company. These activities include visiting certain pages or performing certain searches. Display advertising reaches cold audiences and directs them to a website. Opportunities to target cold audiences in Display advertising include demographic targeting, such as targeting by age or gender, and targeting interested people or people with purchase intentions using Google's data.

Warm audiences, on the other hand, are made up of people who have visited the company's website or purchased the company's products in the past. Returning these people to your website is usually the most profitable part of Google Display advertising. Warm audiences are made up of all the visitors who return to the website, as well as people who have completed microconversions, such as those who have watched a video. With warm audiences, advertising can be targeted to visitors who have visited your website within a month, browsed a certain page, or browsed a certain page for a certain period of time and then returned to your website and completed a certain conversion goal.

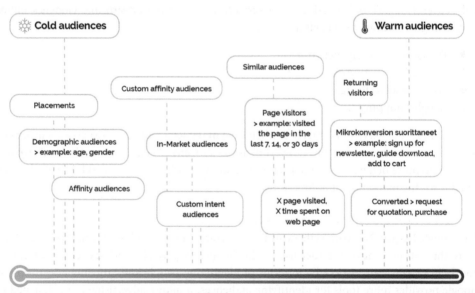

Figure 5.15   Targeting ads to cold and warm audiences

Display advertising can be targeted very precisely to a wide variety of audiences. Google already has a huge number of ready-made audiences, and it has been said, for example, that when someone was dating her partner, Google had known about her intentions long before the person began dating her partner, based on the person's search behavior. In addition, the company can customize audiences based on its own data.

In display advertising, as in all other advertising, it is important to consider the stage of the person's purchase process. The same ad should not be shown to the same audiences all the time, the ad should change according to the online behavior of Internet users. We will next go through how to do display advertising at the different stages of the buying process (Figure 5.16).

Customer stage on buying process	Ad message	Landing page		
				EXAMPLE
Problem	Focus on customer's problem	Low-level secondary conversion	>	Reads blog post till the end
				EXAMPLE
Information search	Guiding customer and giving information	Secondary conversion	>	Guide download
				EXAMPLE
Selection & comparison	Highlighting benefits of the company's product or service	Conversion	>	Demo signup, reading reference stories
				EXAMPLE
Decision	Encouraging the purchase of the product or service	Primary conversion (product or service page)	>	Request for quotation, purchase

Figure 5.16   Planning for display advertising at the different stages of the buying process

- *At the stage of arousing interest and solving the problem,* potential customers who are not yet familiar with the company's brand or products are targeted. The goal is to make your ad as accessible as possible to as many people as possible and to gather a remarketing list of all the people who have shown a genuine interest in the ad. The aim is not to direct a potential customer directly to making a request for a quotation, but to get him or her to read, for instance, a blog article to the end and get to know the website in more detail. As with first dates: first, greetings are exchanged, and marriage is not immediately proposed. Still, the advertisement should not be blindly targeted at all possible audiences but at genuine potential customers in a cost-effective manner and utilizing previous customer information.
  - Targeting: Custom affinity audiences and similar audiences.
  - Advertised content: General blog posts on "Did You Know That?" articles. The aim of the content is to arouse interest and highlight a possible problem of the customer that the customer does not yet know exists.
- *The information retrieval phase* is aimed at customers who are already looking for information about the products offered by the company. The targeting used in advertising is based on the remarketing list created at an earlier stage (i.e., people who have shown interest in the company's products are targeted). The goal is to guide the customer forward on their purchasing path and get her or him to learn more about the product. Suitable content for the information retrieval phase is, for example, buyer's guides that gather the contact information of those who download the guide—this information can be used later for email marketing.

- Targeting: All users in the previous step who read the whole blog post or visited the company's website are targeted. To keep the targeting from being too low, it will also be extended to in-market audiences who have recently shown interest in the product. In this way, the message is delivered both as remarketing to those who have seen the previous ad and to new people who are already aware of their needs but do not yet know about the company's products.
- Advertised content: Buyer's guides.

- *In the selection and comparison phase,* the customer is already aware of their needs and actively compares different service providers. The goal of advertising in this phase is to take the customer forward on his or her buying path and get him or her to choose the company that just advertised from among all the competitors.
  - Targeting: People who have downloaded a buyer's guide.
  - Advertised content: Product information pages, price information, reference stories, financing, a photo gallery.

- *In the decision phase,* the customer looks for the best possible solution or service to meet her or his needs. At this point, she or he is already ready to make a request for a quotation and work out a final price with the seller. The targeting targets a very warm audience, so we can already talk about real targeted marketing. The ad directs the potential buyer towards submitting a request for a quotation.
  - Targeting: All the visitors involved in the previous stage who read more detailed information about the products, examined the price information, and got acquainted with the presentation of the company are targeted.
  - Advertised content: A free consultation page that explains the benefits of a consultation visit. A request-a-quote page for customers who already know exactly what they want.

5.3.3.2   Google Discovery advertising

Discovery advertising is advertising on the Google Discover platform. In the MRACE® model, it focuses on the Reach and Convert steps. The Discover platform includes the Google Discover Feed, Gmail, and YouTube. The Discover Feed is the feed of news and advertisements that Google brings to the user in the context of Google's mobile app.

Discovery advertising is similar in style to social media advertising and has been seen as Google's counterweight to Facebook and Instagram advertising. Discovery ads appear on Google's Discover platform, like native ads among news articles, so users do not get bored of banners in the same way as they do on many news sites and they have less ads to process. Discovery ads also do not look like ads, which is why they often have high click-through rates. This is also due to the fact that the ad content displayed to each user is based on user activity on Google services and recent interests.

Discovery advertising quickly became a popular form of advertising in 2020, not only because of the good results it offers, but also because it is straightforward to get started. All you need is a few images and captions to get started advertising. Your ads will then be shown to interested customers based on your cost per action (CPA) and budget. Discovery campaigns can reach up to 2.9 billion customers on popular Google feeds. The large size of the audience also means that advertising needs to be targeted wisely so that the budget is not wasted in an instant.

Google Display and Discovery ads are often compared because they have very similar policies and targeting patterns. However, Display ads only appear on the Google Display Network, for instance, in websites and apps. With Discovery advertising, your advertising is much more visible in Google's services: the Discovery Feed, Gmail, and YouTube (Figure 5.17). This makes Discovery advertising more multi-channel, relevant, and effective. Discovery advertising therefore benefits every organization when it is done properly. It can be used in both B2C and B2B industries, in recruitment advertising, in the advertising of blog articles, and in the acquisition of leads (e.g., by advertising a guide or webinar). Discovery advertising is also a good option when your SEM clicks are high.

In the Reach phase, Discovery advertising works very well for increasing brand awareness because the ads are visual, inspiring, and based on user interest and behavior. Therefore, an ad seen on the Google Discovery Network will feel very relevant and appropriate to the user, especially if the ad is well produced. Discovery campaigns make it possible to arouse the interest of potential customers before they begin the information retrieval phase in their purchasing process. This allows the company to connect with a potential customer before its competitors.

Figure 5.17   Multi-channel Discovery advertising

In the Convert phase, Discovery advertising works best when you want to reach your most important customers again. When consumers return to search for content on their favorite Google feeds, Discovery campaigns can increase the number of conversions among customers who know the brand best and are more likely to stay active.

In Discovery advertising, the possibilities for targeting your ads are very similar to those of other Google advertising technologies. Advertising can use Google's ready-made audiences that it has created in order for advertisers to take advantage of the vast amount of data it collects. In addition, audiences can be customized based on the advertiser's needs, which gives advertising more opportunities to stand out from the competition.

A very simple way to implement advertising targeting is to divide your audiences into the above-mentioned cold and warm audiences. In many cases, the company gets the fastest visible results from warm audiences, but in the long run, they may not be better than the results from cold audiences. The potential of Discovery advertising to increase brand awareness among cold audiences is high, which can yield significant results in the longer term. That is why data integrity, its interpretation, conclusions, and testing are essential parts of Discovery advertising (like all other digital marketing).

For achieving the best results, Discovery ads should also be designed to support the customer's purchase process and targeted at the right place on the customer's purchase path. For example, if you are very stressed without being aware of it, you should see an advert for an article about the harm of stress or telling you how to eliminate stress. In contrast, your interest could be aroused by an ad addressing topics that you can identify with, such as an article entitled "Do you sleep worse than before? Five tips on how to get better sleep" that explains that stress can cause sleep disorders. In this way, for example, a company that offers meditation courses gets the attention of its potential customer. If the customer has not yet noticed the meditation guide offered by the company on his or her first visit, the company can advertise it through Discovery advertising with the title "Five minutes of meditation will give you half an hour of deeper sleep."

Targeting Discovery advertising at different stages of the buying process can be summarized as follows. Once a customer has just identified her or his problem or need, he or she should be targeted by adverts for a relevant product or service. In the information retrieval phase, the customer is actively looking for a solution to his or her problem, so he or she should be provided with more information related to solving the problem. In the selection and comparison phase, the company should emphasize the benefits of its product in advertising as the customer compares different products. In the final decision stage, it is worth encouraging the customer to buy the product, for example, by raising the benefits of the product or by telling good customer stories in advertising (Figure 5.18).

	Customer stage on buying process	Ad message	Landing page		
R	Problem	Focus on customer's problem	Low-level secondary conversion	>	ESIM. Reads blog post till the end
C	Information search	Guiding customer and giving information	Secondary conversion	>	ESIM. Guide download
C	Selection & comparison	Highlighting benefits of the company's product or service	Conversion	>	ESIM. Demo signup, reading reference stories
C	Decision	Encouraging the purchase of the product or service	Primary conversion (product or service page)	>	ESIM. Request for quotation, purchase

Figure 5.18 Discovery advertising in different stages of the buying process

5.3.3.3   YouTube advertising

YouTube advertising is used to promote a company's brand and product. It adheres very well to the principles of Display advertising. Their target audiences are similar, and both channels direct visitors to the landing page best suited for advertising. The absolute benefits of YouTube advertising are that video can communicate things that cannot be done with images and text alone. On the other hand, video is slower to edit than either image- or text-based advertising, so videos need to be carefully designed.

YouTube is the world's most popular website and, according to several rankings, the world's second largest search engine. In addition, Google is increasingly placing relevant video results in the list of Google searches. As a result, high-quality, regular video production that provides useful information to its potential customers also helps your company's search engine visibility in Google services. Excellent video content is content in which the company answers the most common questions from its customers as the purchase process for many products or services is very long, so there are a lot of questions.

YouTube is not just a video service for teens; people over 35 are the fastest growing user base on YouTube. Therefore, the question is: What kind of video content can a company use to attract the interest of its potential customers on YouTube? Once the issue is resolved and a high-quality video is made to target a specific activity, YouTube advertising will be easier to target. If a video does not have a clear goal and is not designed specifically for YouTube, it will be very difficult to get results with YouTube advertising.

At its best, YouTube advertising occurs in the Reach phase of the MRACE® model, where product or service videos that focus directly on the problem work best. Such videos first present a solution to a customer's problem and only then explain the benefits of the product or service. In the Reach phase, product videos that focus solely on providing the solution and its benefits can also be used. The main goal of video advertising is therefore to arouse interest and make the brand known.

YouTube advertising can also be used a little bit more sophistically to generate leads and thus promote sales. In generating leads, a typical tactic is to advertise downloadable content, such as guides. Act- and Convert-stage videos are suitable for lead generation, where the goal is to get the viewer to perform some desired action before the actual transaction.

The easiest way to approach YouTube advertising that is solely meant for the Convert phase (i.e., advertising directed to a straight transaction) is with a video that has a clear offer and encourages you to buy right away. By only using YouTube advertising, it is difficult to make sales, but advertisers who take advantage of YouTube and SEM at the same time have an average conversion rate that is 3 percent higher than advertisers who take advantage of SEM alone. Such a large difference in the conversion rate has a clear impact on business. YouTube advertising strongly supports other marketing channels and enables highly visual advertising for a precisely segmented audience.

Targeting YouTube advertising is remarkably effective compared with TV advertising, for example. YouTube advertising can target a specific audience based on a user's specific interests (such as custom or Google-ready audience ratings) but also based on a user's location, age, or a combination of these. The targeting of video ads on YouTube is very similar to that of Display advertising, but on YouTube, the advertising can also be targeted to, among other things, life events. For example, advertising can be targeted at people who have set up a business. Video ads can also be targeted to a specific YouTube channel or in relation to an individual video; similarly, certain channels can be excluded from targeting.

When used properly, YouTube advertising is a powerful tool for remarketing. It is a good idea to target users who have previously visited your organization's website or its YouTube channel, for example. Advertising to such an audience is typically effective and relatively inexpensive as advertising is better received by a warm audience than it is by a cold audience, so advertising to a warm audience is more likely to bring about results. Remarketing can also engage existing customers with the company. It acts as so-called top-of-mind marketing (i.e., marketing that keeps the brand in mind for a potential or current customer).

Utilization of YouTube advertising can be roughly divided into the following four main categories, depending on the industry and need of the business: brand advertising, product or service advertising, lead generation, and remarketing (Figure 5.19). The optimal campaign structure takes advantage of multiple categories of these, allowing video content to be targeted to people at different stages of the buying path.

Figure 5.19   Using YouTube advertising

YouTube is great for brand advertising because it allows a company to increase its brand awareness and strengthen its brand image. Pre-roll ads that last 5 seconds can be precisely targeted to the desired audience, and the viewer can continue to watch longer if the video catches her or his attention. Pre-roll ads run on YouTube before the actual video.

It is recommended that you use both long and short videos to promote your product or service. Long videos are apt to guide and teach the customer about the company's product. In this case, the benefits of the product should be presented to the customer during the first few seconds so that the customer becomes interested and she or he clicks on the company's website. Product demos can be implemented in a shorter format and can direct the customer to go to the website to continue the purchasing process. Product and service advertising uses either Reach- or Act-phase videos, depending on the business of the company and the information needs of the customers.

Generating new content or marketing a webinar, for example, are commonly used to generate leads. Leads can also be generated by using offers with precise targeting in order to get the offers to the right customers. Act- and Convert-stage videos are suitable for lead generation.

Remarketing is at its most effective in top-of-mind marketing, as well as in engaging customers with a service. By using top-of-mind marketing, a brand remains well known and is kept in the mind of the potential customer. This is especially important for companies whose product is purchased frequently. Top-of-mind marketing is also useful in long purchasing processes because the more often a customer encounters a company while the purchasing process is in progress, the more familiar and reliable the company begins to feel.

The customer's commitment to the service is most likely when the purchase decision is still fresh because then the customer will be the most likely to receive and process marketing communications from the brand. The targeting of post-purchase videos is based on conversion data collected from the website, and the video is designed so that it supports serving the customer, while at the same time taking into account additional sales opportunities.

5.3.3.4 Optimizing SEA and online advertising

Implementing SEA and online advertising is an ongoing process that needs to be improved on a weekly basis by optimizing advertising. Advertising optimization consists of four important parts: data collection, analysis of results, taking the necessary actions, and concrete development (Figure 5.20). Data is constantly accumulated as advertising is done. The data shows, for example, which campaigns are performing best, to what pages directed visitors bring the best results, and which pages are performing the worst. The results are analyzed from the perspective of the collected data and advertising is developed on the basis of the analysis.

Advertising development includes monitoring cost-effectiveness and optimizing it, familiarizing yourself with search terms, finding new keywords and adding negative keywords, A/B testing of ads, testing new targeting methods, creating ad extensions, experimenting with campaigns, following competitive situations, and responding to competition. For example, if you find that people who search with certain keywords never convert to making a purchase, you should remove those keywords from your advertising and move that media budget to well-performing keywords.

With the continuous development of advertising, advertising becomes cost-effective. If advertising is just built up and then forgotten, its quality will decline, it will incur a lot of unnecessary costs, and your keyword ads will show less well on Google's search results page. The ever-changing competitive situation then drives competitors to gain higher placing on the search results page.

Data and AI also play an increasingly important role in the development of advertising. Historical data and AI software enable you to quickly process large amounts of data so that they are saved in your campaign's change history for later review. The utilization of machine learning and AI will only become relevant in advertising when sufficient data has been collected from advertising. In some smaller industries in Finland, machine learning can only be used to a very limited extent because Finland's search volumes are very small compared with countries with a larger population.

However, if advertising does not bring good results, the poor results are not always due to the quality of the advertising and can also be due to a poor website. Websites and landing pages should be developed when the site or page receives a lot of traffic through advertising but the traffic does not result in purchases or contact requests. In this case, the advertising works, but the website or landing page does not do its job.

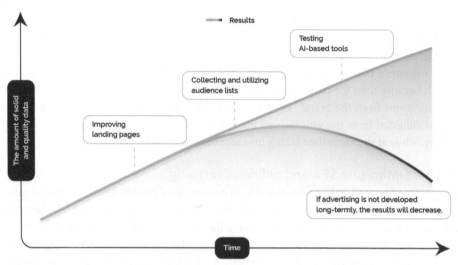

Figure 5.20   The competitive situation: the market and the tools are constantly changing, which is why the performance curve of advertising built on the "build and leave to roll" principle points downwards

LämpöYkkönen is a company specializing in energy renovation and the energy efficiency optimization of homes and properties. It generates savings for its customers and improves the competitiveness and profitability of customer companies through energy efficiency. The company's vision is to produce the same amount of renewable energy with its customers as a large nuclear power plant by 2030. Because LämpöYkkönen is a sales organization, the success of salespeople largely determines the company's growth rate.

HOW DO YOU INCREASE THE EFFECTIVENESS OF YOUR SALES ORGANIZATION THROUGH MARKETING?

Salespeople are most time efficient when they talk to a ready-to-buy customer. It is even better if the customer does not talk to any competing company at the same time. Based on this idea, LämpöYkkönen's marketing function generated four main goals:

1. Reaching a potential customer before she or he even thinks about energy renovation because at that stage she or he has not started a conversation with competitors (this covers the Reach stage).
2. Increasing customers' trust in LämpöYkkönen, which increases the company's attractiveness at every meeting point between the customer and the company (this covers the Reach, Act, and Convert stages).
3. Generating as many good quotes as possible for salespeople so that they can focus on selling instead of nurturing cold leads or focusing on customer prospecting (this covers the Convert stage).
4. Harnessing existing customers to add value to potential new customers. References and satisfied customers are the most effective ways of marketing (this covers the Engage and Reach stages).

HOW WERE THE GOALS ACHIEVED?

Three issues were brought to the forefront of the Reach phase: organic social media (i.e., postings published on the company's social media channels), SEO, and paid advertising on Google. Content that aroused interest and reactions was chosen as the main focus on social media. Organic content was then easy to boost with paid advertising because the hardest part is creating good content, not distributing it.

With the help of social media, LämpöYkkönen reached customers who had not yet even considered energy renovation. Instead, through SEO and Google's paid and personalized advertising, they caught customers who had embarked on an active buying process and were looking for information or a partner to support it.

When the Reach phase generates a lot of visitors to a website, it needs to run smoothly and direct visitors towards a call for a quotation, otherwise the visitors will not benefit the company. That is why the site invested in CRO so that visitors could quickly request a quote from any page. In addition, the personalized content for the information retrieval phase (the Act phase) and the purchase phase (the Convert phase) was carefully designed using, for example, heatmaps: they showed how visitors behaved on the website, what they were paying attention to, and what important things the visitors did not notice. The more customers know and independently search for information to support their purchasing decision, the more they are ready-made leads for sales.

Information retrieval and purchasing decisions were also supported by marketing automation, wherein each contact was provided with personalized content based on his or her behavior. In addition, existing customers were harnessed to acquire new customers through a referral program.

A FEW KEY FIGURES

REACH

The amount of organic traffic from search engines increased by 29 percent compared with the previous year.

ACT

A survey aimed at customers and leads generated more than 300 different questions that led to the creation of more than 100 blog articles.

CONVERT

The number of invitations to tender received through organic transport increased by 87 percent compared with the previous year.

The number of requests for quotations received through SEM increased by 80 percent, although only 3 percent more money was spent than in the previous year.

ENGAGE

The size of the email list increased by 12,000 contacts in six months.

5.4   MARKETING AUTOMATION AND EMAIL MARKETING

As stated, *marketing automation* refers to the automated distribution of content to customers and the scaling of personalized marketing. Marketing automation systems can be used for collecting customer-related data and for segmenting firms' contacts based on data and sending them relevant and timely messages. When a customer responds to messages as desired or when she or he performs desired actions on the site, salespeople can contact her or him to inquire if she or he needs help with any matter. Thus, marketing automation plays a significant role in the digital sales process. Despite its name, the adoption of marketing automation does not fully automate marketing or reduce the amount of time or money invested in it—it eliminates routine work and frees up time from segmentation and content distribution for content creation and strategic planning. In the MRACE® model, marketing automation primarily affects the Convert and Engage phases. In the Convert phase, more leads can be turned into deals, and in the Engage phase, the existing customer base is engaged via relevant communications.

The importance of personalized marketing is also emphasized in the digital environment. You only click on a link, read an email, or watch a video if they (a) come to you at the right time and (b) arouse your immediate interest. Marketing automation opens a channel for the company in which marketing is timely, personalized, measurable, and automated. Personalization cannot be overemphasized: for example, you can imagine that if a cat owner constantly receives messages from a pet store about dog food or dog-related things, he will not continue to subscribe to that company's newsletter for very long. In contrast, if he were to constantly receive personalized messages about cats, he would be more likely to welcome them (Figure 5.21).

The importance of marketing automation is emphasized when a company uses paid advertising from which it wants to make the most profit. Only about 1–3 percent of site visitors are

Figure 5.21   The more precisely segmented an email list is, the more relevant marketing
a company can do

willing to talk to the company in more detail when they visit the company's website. If the company does not offer any lighter conversion points, such as the opportunity to download a guide or attend a webinar, to the other visitors to its site, up to 99 percent of the traffic has been wasted. If, in turn, a company gets some visitors to download a guide or otherwise leave their contact information, they end up in the realm of marketing automation where these contacts are nurtured in order to become sales-ready leads. The cost-effectiveness of paid advertising is enormously improved in this way.

5.4.1   How can a company acquire contacts for the marketing automation domain?

Contacts are the fuel of marketing automation. If a company is not able to add contacts to the marketing automation domain, it is a mere expense and of no benefit to the company. Therefore, you need to invest in making contacts.

The most typical way to do this is to use the various *lead magnets* (i.e., the targeted content that is directed at potential customers when they give the company their contact information, such as their email address or phone number). Examples of lead magnets include webinars, webinar recordings, downloadable guides, e-books, online magazines, and downloadable reference stories. Contacts can also be made for marketing automation, for example, through pop-ups, raffles, chatbots, and newsletter subscription forms. Once the company has created sufficient methods to acquire contacts into the marketing automation domain, the actual marketing automation process may begin.

Imagine a person visiting a company's website for the first time and deciding to subscribe to a newsletter by entering her email address. At this point, the company knows little about the contact, such as what product or service the contact is interested in or why she subscribed to the newsletter in the first place. However, with the help of marketing automation, it is possible to start finding out about this person's background and areas of interest. The moment she sent her email address to the company using the subscription form for the newsletter, a cookie was placed in her browser. The marketing automation system can then see what she does on the company's website: which subpages she visits, whether she opens the emails sent by the company, and whether or not she clicks on their links.

Subscribing to a newsletter also triggers an automated series of emails that have two functions: to familiarize the company with the contact and to find out what interests the contact. Such an automated series of emails typically last from a week to a month, depending on how the contact responds to the emails he or she receives. You can think of this type of automation as a situation similar to arriving at a shoe department in a sports shop, for example. The seller greets you, briefly tells you about the company and the selection, and asks what kind of shoes you are looking for. You tell him or her that you need new running shoes, and then you start looking for the right shoes with the seller.

In marketing automation, the equivalent process proceeds by presenting the company and its range of offerings in emails. When a contact clicks on a link in an email related to a certain product and is directed to a relevant web page, this already indicates that he or she is interested in that product. If he or she also reads other content on the site about the same product, the marketing system will learn that he or she is interested in the product. This event launches interest-based automation that aims to tell the contact more about the product, help the contact solve his or her problems, and transfer the most engaged contacts to the salespeople. In this way, the subscriber of the newsletter becomes a potential and identified sales opportunity.

However, marketing automation will not work without a sufficient amount of content. If a company's pages only have one service page and a few blog articles about one service, the content is not enough at all. Why? Such a scarcity of content means that the marketing automation system is unable to identify whether or not the contact is interested in buying from the company. If a contact can only read one article about the offering provided by a company, the system cannot say whether or not the contact who visited this page twice was interested or not. In contrast, if a company has dozens of different articles about their service and a contact reads half of them, the system will immediately recognize that the contact is clearly interested in that service.

In addition, the role of marketing automation is to provide the right content to your contacts at the right time. If there is no content, automation has nothing to offer to the contacts. Content pieces must also cover the entire purchase path (from the beginning to the end). Content in the early stages of the path includes articles that focus on the customer's problem. Content in the later stages of the path includes well-made reference stories and service or product pages.

5.4.1.1   Segmentation revolutionizes the effectiveness of marketing automation

It is possible to segment contacts based on demographic information and contact behavior. Segmentation works best when the two methods are combined. This makes emails and campaigns feel much more personal and relevant to the recipient.

A commonly used method of segmenting contacts is to divide them into a square diagram with a vertical axis from A to D and a horizontal axis from 1 to 4, resulting in 16 squares in total (Figure 5.22). In the graph, the A–D axis represents how good the contact appears based on demographic data. A is the best and D is the worst. For example, A could be senior management, B middle management, C an expert, and D a student. The 1–4 axis, in turn, represents how active the contact has been recently. The most active level is rated as 1, and the most passive level is rated as 4. The A1 contacts are thus the best and the D4 contacts the worst.

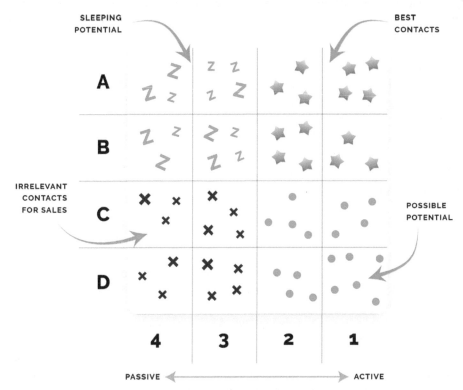

Figure 5.22   Contact segmentation in marketing automation

With clearly segmented contacts, it is easy to send them personalized campaigns. The marketing approach of the email should be completely different for a student interested in the company than for a marketing director interested in the company. It is easy for sales to use their resources to only contact certain contacts, such as those categorized as A1–A3 or those categorized as B1–B2. In this case, each conversation is held with a relevant and recently active contact. The seller will also be notified whenever a new contact reaches one of the above segments. In this case, the time spent on sales prospecting and other routine work is reduced.

Thanks to segmentation and automatic profiling, the seller also knows the contact a little before the first contact. The seller can see from the contact's profile what content he or she has read and which topics are clearly of interest to him or her. Customer services can also take advantage of the data generated by marketing automation in a similar way, allowing the customer service representative to serve the contact much more personally.

Via Tribunali is Finland's first certified Neapolitan pizzeria. The art of Neapolitan pizza-makers is on UNESCO's Intangible Cultural Heritage List, and certificates are issued by the True Neapolitan Pizza Association.

The primary goal of Via Tribunal's marketing has been to teach Finnish consumers to understand the difference between a high-quality Neapolitan pizza and an "ordinary" pizza and thus create appreciation of high-quality pizza. The ways in which Neapolitan pizza is made differ significantly from what many are used to in terms of the ingredients and the taste. The whole of their marketing is built around the following question: How can something as familiar as pizza sound so new and exciting that everyone wants to try it?

HOW WERE CUSTOMERS EDUCATED TO BUY SOMETHING NEW?

Via Tribunali brought Neapolitan pizza to Finland. The market was therefore completely new and customers did not really realize they would need this product. For this reason, the most important thing was to tell customers why a Neapolitan pizza is different and better than the pizzas the customer knows. Therefore, a decision was made to focus strongly on the Reach and Act phases in order to increase market awareness and interest.

The heart of the marketing was formed of a variety of downloadable recipe books that teach customers how to make Neapolitan-style pizza at home. With downloadable materials, Via Tribunali has succeeded in adding value to its target audience and teaching how Neapolitan pizza differs from regular pizza. At the same time, Via Tribunal's mailing list has grown significantly, creating a direct connection for the company to its customer base.

Three spearheads were chosen to feature in the communication, which appear in recipe books, social media advertisements, and in the contents of the Via Tribunali's website: a 450-degree (Celsius) oven and a 60-second baking time, a delicious dough that has risen for 20 hours, and carefully selected ingredients. When one of these communication spearheads is always highlighted, the distinctiveness of Neapolitan pizza remains in the minds of customers and the product awareness of the target group grows.

HOW SHOULD MARKETING DEVELOP IN THE FUTURE?

The awareness of Finnish people about Neapolitan pizza has grown a lot in recent years. When the market is new, "technical" features (like a 450-degree oven) sound exciting and raise interest. As the market evolves, product features begin to become self-evident because customers are already familiar with them. That is why Via Tribunali has increasingly shifted the focus of its marketing to the brand and its appeal, as well as to the creation of a customer community. In this way, the company is ready to take the market maturity and product awareness to the next level as it always requires a change in the marketing approach as well.

A FEW KEY FIGURES

REACH

Social media advertising reached 329,936 people in six months.

ACT

The website's Menu page was visited by 13,776 visitors during six months.

CONVERT

The company has an ever-growing mailing list of about 10,000 subscribers.

5.5   SOCIAL MEDIA MARKETING

There are numerous different platforms on social media upon which a company can produce content and advertise. The social networking service Facebook is the largest social platform with almost three billion users. The number of Facebook users has decreased among younger people, but in turn, has increased among those over 45 years of age.

The image-sharing service Instagram has almost 1.5 billion users, while the rapidly growing video-sharing service TikTok has exceeded over one billion users. There are about 740 million LinkedIn users in the world, while Snapchat has about 600 million, Twitter about 500 million, and Pinterest about 400 million users.

In this book, we will primarily cover social media marketing from the perspectives of Facebook, Instagram, and LinkedIn, as the potential for doing paid advertising on these channels is the most advanced and established. At the time of writing this book, for example, TikTok advertising has only just become available in Finland.

At a general level, social media marketing involves an ongoing optimization of ad content, the audience, and the advertising budget as designing an advertising message for the target audience is critical to advertising effectiveness. At the heart of social media marketing is knowing the advertising's target audience. This knowledge of the target group grows as data accumulates from advertising; you can see which messages interest the target group the most, and this data can be used to make advertising more effective. With machine learning solutions, campaigns can be optimized around the clock and AI can automatically increase its budget, for example, when there are more conversions than normal.

The unified and recognizable look of a brand is emphasized on social media as one of the important goals of social media advertising is to increase brand awareness while generating leads and generating interest. The social media budgets of large companies easily reach more than €10,000 a month, and especially with such a large investment, the advertising space must definitely look coherent, interesting, and recognizable. It not only creates clarity and confidence in the customer's mind, but also produces a better result in terms of the figures (see also Section 5.2.3). However, not every potential customer is interested in the same ad, which is why you need to create a sufficient number of different ads that can be targeted to different buyer personas.

5.5.1　Social media advertising as part of the MRACE® model

In the MRACE® model, the role of social media advertising is to arouse interest in the company among new target groups and to have people who have already started their purchasing process return to the company's website (e.g., through remarketing). Thus, social media advertising is an important part of the entire MRACE® model, from the Reach stage to the Engage stage.

In the Reach stage, social media advertising is aimed at reaching people who are interested in the company's products or services and creating interest towards the company in completely new target groups. If the target group already knows the company's product or service, you can directly advertise the product or service and its benefits. If the target group does not already know the product or does not know that they need the company's product, the advertising directed at it should focus, for example, on a problem with which the target group identifies themselves as having. If a company sells pillows, an ad for social media could start with the question "Are you sleeping poorly?" or "Is your neck sore when you wake up?" After this, the company can tell a potential customer why this happens and direct her or him to their site, moving her or him towards solving the problem (i.e., buying a new pillow in this case).

In the Reach phase, CPC and the click-through rate are used as the key metrics of social media advertising. It is also advisable to look at the average cost of one thousand ad impressions (the CPM), what kind of a relevance score the ad has received, how many times the ad has been clicked, how many people who clicked on the ad leave the associated landing page immediately, and whether the ad receives comments or likes. These all indicate whether the advertising is well targeted and whether the content resonates with the buyer persona. If a potential customer is directed through an ad to a site where they watch a short video or read a blog post, they may be a relevant audience for Act-stage advertising.

In the Act stage, the target group is familiar with the product or service offered by the company. Therefore, social media advertising can focus on showcasing the benefits of a product or service as well as its ability to solve a problem experienced by a customer. In the Act phase, it is important to direct the customer from ads to website content that provides comprehensive additional information that will support the purchase decision as in the Act phase the customer wants to compare service providers and find out if the product or service offered by the company is best for her or him. A company that sells pillows could tell you how the material, shape, and stitching of their pillows will help relieve neck pain and for whom each pillow is particularly suitable.

From the Act stage onwards, measuring social media advertising will no longer focus as much on the internal metrics of the social media platforms but will focus on what kind of actions the people referred to the site take on the site. In the Act phase, it is a good idea to track microconversions (such as the reading time for blog posts and material downloads) when measuring social media advertising. Clicks on contact information pages also show interest in the company, so they should also be considered. In an online store, adding products to the shopping cart and browsing product pages are good metrics for determining a customer's level of interest.

In the Convert stage, we recommend purely doing product and reference advertising. With advertising, the customer can be directed directly towards making a purchase or requesting an offer because at this stage the customer already knows that the product or service is a potential option for him or her.

The Convert stage measures how many macroconversions—such as requests for a quotation, contact requests, or purchases—have been generated through social media advertising.

In the Engage stage, firms should do top-of-mind advertising for customers as that keeps the company in mind. The purpose of this is to engage the customer with the company's brand and strengthen the customer's sense of a good purchasing decision. In addition, in the Engage stage, you may want to promote content that will help your customer learn to use your product better or more often.

The Engage stage measures how many repurchases, product reviews, company reviews, references, and returning customers to a website are generated through social media advertising.

Please note that the social media ads for the different stages of the MRACE® model are not rigid in style and communication. Often, for example, advertising that uses customer testimonials is a great way to both gain new customers in the Reach phase and engage existing customers in the Engage phase.

5.5.2   Influencer marketing

Have you ever wondered if your company should partner with social media influencers? Utilizing influencers in marketing is a very relevant and topical issue and has also attracted the interest of marketing researchers. In the MRACE® model, influencer marketing can significantly increase the awareness of a company and its offerings in the Reach phase. In addition, the product reviews and user experiences made by influencers are content that supports the purchase decision in the Convert phase.

The majority of influencer marketing research gives a positive picture of the meaningfulness of influencer marketing. In 2019, a survey was conducted involving 600 Americans who followed at least one influencer on social media. In the survey, 70 percent of participants trusted influencers as much or more than the opinions of their friends, and 78 percent trusted the content produced by influencers more than advertisements. According to the survey, more than half of the respondents considered influencers as their friends. In addition, almost 80 percent of the respondents had purchased a product due to a post published by an influencer. On the other hand, according to the world's largest influencer marketing survey,[1] only 4 percent of Internet users trust what influencers say online.

According to various sources, influencer marketing is considered to be the most effective form of advertising. Half of consumers say influencers guide their purchasing decisions. About 70 percent of marketers say that influencer marketing has helped them reach their target audience effectively. The trend in influencer marketing is to use influencers over a longer period of time, not just in one campaign. The most important thing in influencer marketing cooperation is the similarity of the values of the company and those of the influencer who is advertising the company—the fit of the influencer to the context of the advertised product is crucial.

Influencer marketing has grown exponentially in recent years and is projected to generate more than €20 billion of business in 2023. However, nearly half of marketers spend less than 5 percent of their marketing budget on influencer collaboration. The popularity of influencer marketing is likely to grow as customers value UGC more and more in the midst of a constant flood of advertising.

Of the euros spent on influencer marketing, the lion's share has gone to cooperation with the biggest so-called macro influencers, such as footballer Cristiano Ronaldo and the reality TV family the Kardashians. However, the influencer marketing industry predicts that cooperation will turn more and more towards micro-influencer cooperation. Companies are looking for collaborators who have relatively few followers on social media, typically less than 10,000, but who are significant and followed by a certain limited target group.

These micro influencers are effectively identified through social media monitoring, which shows, for example, the people who have written and commented the most on a particular forum, such as on LinkedIn. In addition, nano influencers with less than 1,000 followers can be distinguished from micro influencers. Nano influencers are unknown to the general public but are well known in, for example, sports and hobby circles, which makes them valuable partners for companies. Today, there are also several websites through which influencers are recruited, suggesting the proliferation and growth of influencer marketing.

The most popular social media influencers in Finland are, for example, Mmiisas, Lakko, Mariieveronica, Hermanni, Roni Bäck, and PewDiePie. The last one, PewDiePie was reported to have earned €14 million in 2014 from his influencer cooperations, mainly in the video game industry. Today, many influencers in the digital world are also heavily featured in traditional media, such as on television, making them more widely known to the general public.

One interesting future scenario for influencer marketing is the use of virtual influencers. A *virtual influencer* is an invented character used in influencer marketing. The virtual influencer can be like an ordinary person or like a cartoon character. There is still relatively little research on virtual influencers, so we will not discuss the phenomenon further here.

5.5.3   Product reviews online

Closely related to influencer marketing are product reviews collected on e-commerce websites or on social media. They have a strong impact in the Convert phase, when the customer is still considering making a purchase decision. As we mentioned at the beginning of the book, recommendation is a significant factor in attracting customers and speeding up purchasing processes.

However, product reviews also have their downsides. In 2018, the *Washington Post* published an article[2] alleging that half of Amazon's product reviews were fake. According to the article, it is hard to sell anything through Amazon today if you play an honest game. If you want your product to be competitive with Amazon's huge offering, you have to start falsifying product reviews. According to Amazon itself, 99 percent of their product reviews are real because they are written by real buyers who have not been paid anything.

However, paying for product reviews has been commonplace for both online stores and many other players. In the context of product reviews, it would be important to tell other customers if the product review was based on a reward or free product in a similar manner to online advertising content (such as that created by influencers) that must have a #ad tag.

An important question for the credibility of digital marketing is how many of the ratings are true ratings, how many are bought with money, and how many are created by robots. Is the digital marketing world shooting itself in the foot by tarnishing its reputation with fake product reviews?

Product reviews have a significant impact on the visibility of products on Google and an online store's own search engines. The better the reviews and the more reviews a product has received, the better search visibility it usually has. Thus, falsified reviews entice many companies to act unethically. A similar phenomenon is observed in increasing the number of social media followers as money can be used to buy social media followers. For example, it is estimated that around half of many celebrities' followers on Twitter might be fake.[3] Confidence in the accuracy of online content is one of the biggest problems with digital marketing as the threshold for publishing content online is just a click.

CASE STUDY
CASE EXAMPLE: SOCIAL MEDIA ADVERTISING AS A DRIVER OF 24RENT.FI'S GROWTH

In Finland, 24Rent.fi is a car sharing service that offers shared cars for both individuals and companies. The cars can always be found close to the customers and can be purchased as a self-service for any length of time and at any time of the day or night.

The goal of 24Rent.fi's marketing has been to increase the utilization rate of cars by acquiring new customers (covering the Reach, Act, and Convert stages) and ensuring the return of existing customers (in the Engage stage). The challenge for the company has been that almost the entire customer base, from consumers to companies, has not been aware of the existence of shared cars, and a large proportion of customers have sought a car rental or leasing service. The identification of the challenge has created a direct opportunity to increase the market share of shared cars by acquiring new customers from the target groups of car rental and leasing services.

HOW DID THE NEW SERVICE GAIN A MARKET SHARE FROM TRADITIONAL SERVICES?

When people are not searching for a particular product or service, it must be taken to potential customers. In the case of 24Rent.fi, paid advertising on social media and Google (in the Reach stage) played a key role in reaching potential customers. It was also considered important that the advertising is personalized and precisely targeted in order to make it more effective.

The targeting and personalization were taken to such an advanced level that a potential customer saw the price, availability, and location of a nearby 24Rent.fi car when they opened Facebook or searched for information on Google. This kind of hyper-targeted advertising produced excellent results, especially in social media advertising.

Content was also produced for the company's website from a number of different perspectives in order to highlight the benefits of the new service to different buyer personas (covering the Act and Convert stages). For one buyer persona, price is the most important factor, for another, availability is the most important factor, and for a third, the ease of the process is the most important factor. All the benefits of the service must be clearly stated on the website so that the investments made in advertising are not wasted due to the unclear description of the service, especially when the awareness of the service is increased.

A FEW KEY FIGURES

REACH

Social media advertising reached 536,231 people in six months.
Ads were viewed on social media 3.8 million times in six months.

ACT

Social media advertising directed 22,600 people to the site in six months.

CONVERT

The ROAS of social media advertising was up to 1,345 percent over six months.

5.6   ANALYTICS AND MEASUREMENT

One of the cornerstones of effective digital marketing is the reliable measurement of its effectiveness. The measurement framework for the MRACE® model covers, at its broadest, all the marketing efforts of a company. At best, the information gathered can be used not only to maximize advertising revenue but also to develop business more holistically. Measurement processes should be integrated into all digital marketing at the earliest possible stage so that the effectiveness can be evaluated over time. The primary goal of measurement is to direct resources to the activities that produce the best results. As a whole, firms should make the marketing channels work together to achieve business goals.

Every marketing campaign is an investment with an expected return. By understanding which channels deliver the best return on investment, decisions can be made about the optimal allocation of your marketing budget. The aim should therefore be to understand the digital business holistically, to select the most appropriate performance indicators for it, and to strive for continuous improvement through testing.

5.6.1 The measurement process

The strategic measurement process consists of the following seven phases: situation analysis, a measurement plan, technical implementation, reporting, analysis, optimization, and business development (Figure 5.23). The *situation analysis* examines the amount of existing data and the reliability of its collection methods. The situation is often that the basic installation of analytics software has been completed but it has not been modified to provide important information to the company beyond providing basic data on pageviews.

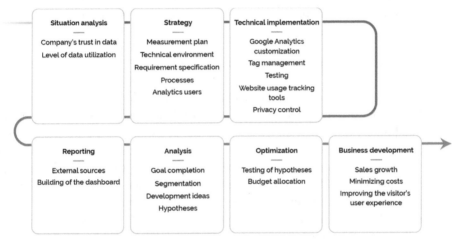

Figure 5.23   The seven steps of a strategic measurement process

After situation analysis, it is vital to determine what information is important and relevant to the company's business. To this end, a *measurement plan* is drawn up that includes the business objectives that are to be monitored and the requirements and details of their technical implementation. All parties involved in marketing are involved in designing the plan as the entire marketing organization must take the measurement requirements into account in the future.

   In the *technical implementation*, the installation of an analytics tool is modified to meet the requirements of the measurement plan, the technical infrastructure, and data protection legislation. The installation takes into account any other information systems that can or must be integrated.

   Reporting provides results that are typically obtained using a browser-based tool that provides up-to-date information about analytics and other connected systems. The dashboard that visualizes the data provides both a general understanding of the digital marketing situation and the more accurate, platform-specific reporting of all the available advertising channels. Therefore, it serves as an effective tool for the various decision makers in an organization.

   In the *analysis* phase, the realization of the objectives defined in the measurement plan is monitored. When interpreting the data, one takes a stand on the ability of different channels to attract potential customers as measured by MRACE® stage metrics. Instead of averages, the most efficient and the weakest customer segments are identified and their strengths and weaknesses are analyzed. By focusing on these, the average figures will also rise. In the *optimization* phase, it is possible to use the information to optimize the functionality of the website, its ability to turn visitors into leads and customers, and the optimal distribution of the budget between different marketing activities, leading to continuous *business development.*

The measurement plan is visible to all parties. It is a good idea to guide marketers to tag incoming links to the website correctly so that the different channels and campaigns can be identified correctly. This is called Urchin Tracking Module (UTM) tagging. Care should be taken to ensure that the data collected by analytics does not contain personal information. In general, we recommend that you keep abreast of evolving data protection laws and, if necessary, respond to any changes.

5.6.2   Managing marketing activities with the MRACE® dashboard

Central to the job of a modern sales and marketing manager is managing operations through the MRACE® dashboard (Figure 5.24). The dashboard shows the ongoing sales and marketing activities and their effectiveness in, for example, lead and transaction generation. Especially when a lot of data is collected, it is a good idea to visualize it according to the MRACE® model on the marketing dashboard: this facilitates sales and marketing management, budgeting, and decision-making. The dashboard keeps you informed about what is happening on the website and with the marketing at the different stages of the MRACE® model. In this way, marketing can be managed in a way that genuinely supports business goals and ensures that marketing euros go where they bring the best results.

When marketing is done in a versatile and multi-channel way, marketing data easily becomes fragmented across different marketing platforms. The marketing dashboard gathers information in one place in an easy-to-interpret visual format, making it easier to perceive the overall picture.

The MRACE® dashboard is backed by Google Data Studio, a data visualization tool developed by Google. With a variety of integration capabilities, the dashboard can be connected to almost any structured data source, starting with a simple Excel spreadsheet. This gives the dashboard all the data you need, and the numbers can be conveniently viewed on a browser on any device. The dashboard also speeds up decision-making as the data is updated in almost real time.

Different users need different key figures to support decision-making. For this reason, several views are built into the dashboard (Figure 5.25):

- There is a *comprehensive managerial overview* that shows what is going on at the different stages of the MRACE® model at a glance. You can also find costs and conversions in this view.
- There is a summary view of marketing channels that makes it easy to compare the results from different marketing channels and identify which marketing channels work best at each stage of the MRACE® model. This helps to outline the customer buying process more holistically.

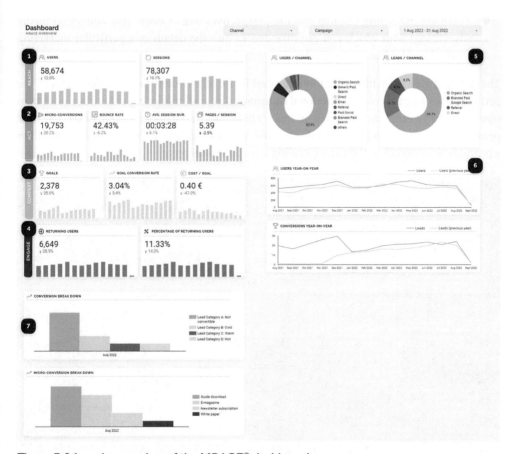

Figure 5.24   An overview of the MRACE® dashboard

Notes: In the Reach phase, we measure how we have reached potential customers, for example, in the form of site visitors and sessions.

In the Act phase, we measure the number and rate of desired actions taken by site visitors: for example, microconversions such as content downloads. Using these metrics, we can also determine the quality of visitor traffic. Act-phase metrics include, for example, average session duration and pages per session.

In the Convert phase, we measure how a site visitor turns into a buying customer. Metrics include, for example, requests for quotations, conversion rate, and cost per acquisition.

In the Engage phase, we measure how visitors and customers engage with the site and the company. Metrics include, for example, returning visitors and the growth of brand searches.

Pie charts show which channels the visitors come from and which channels the conversions in the Convert phase come from.

Trend charts show development in the long term, for example, the development of visitor traffic or the development of the number of requests for quotations.

Conversion breakdowns give insight into the quality of generated leads and show which microconversions have been performed on the website.

● There are marketing channel-specific perspectives (e.g., Google Ads and social media advertising) with which you can dive deeper into the details of a particular marketing channel and look at it in more detail.

The different views and filters built into the dashboard allow you to perceive, for example, the performance of a particular promotional campaign across all marketing channels, rather than trying to get an overall picture based on reports from individual marketing channels. The time period under review can also be easily changed, and the figures can be compared with either a previous time period or the corresponding time period last year.

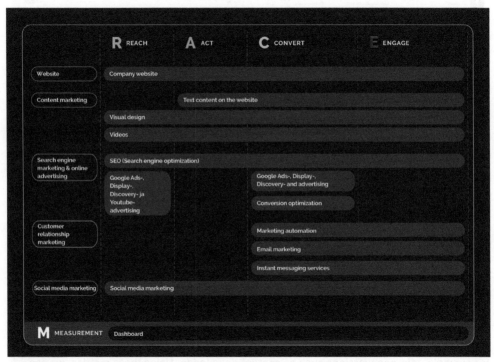

Figure 5.25   Digital marketing channels and tools at different phases

NOTES

1.   UM (2019).
2.   Dwoskin and Timberg (2018).
3.   Boostlikes (2013; updated 2022).

6
Digital marketing work in practice

Competence in digital marketing is now a necessity in marketing work. Companies are hiring people as marketing leaders and experts with titles such as "Digital Marketing Specialist" and "Digital Communications and Marketing Manager." Almost all marketing job postings emphasize the word "digital marketing." Typically, the job description of a person doing or leading digital marketing includes developing and updating an organization's website, producing content on social media channels, and digital advertising. Most often, organizations are looking for people who are also able to report on the results of their digital marketing efforts. The person must have experience and understanding of the use of data and analytics in communication and marketing. As with all marketing work, understanding the topical market trends is one of the key factors in conducting digital marketing.

However, it should be noted that one person cannot manage all the channels of digital marketing so well that she or he could be classified as an expert in all of them. That is why companies seek help from marketing agencies in order to develop marketing and sales. Large-sized marketing agencies usually provide the customer organization with a team of experts, each member of which focuses on improving the performance of only one channel. In such expert agencies, expertise can be illustrated using the so-called T-model (Figure 6.1). The T-model's vertical line describes the depth of the expert's competence in his or her core field, and the horizontal line describes the broad understanding of the entire marketing domain and the influence of other channels on the expert's core working field. In this way, marketing can be managed holistically so that each channel is primarily used for the goal it fits best while the other channels support the same main goal.

6.1   A WEEK IN THE JOURNEY OF A DIGITAL MARKETER: THE MRACE® MODEL AS A TOUR GUIDE

The MRACE® model guides all levels of digital marketing: strategic planning, tactical implementation, and the analysis of results. It is just as suitable for social media advertising and SEO as it is for content production or email automation. Thus, it is a truly holistic way to see the digital marketing as a whole rather than as individual, perhaps competing, channels. When the MRACE® model is combined with agile project- and customer-relationship management models, many pitfalls in customer work can be bypassed, such as wasted advertising euros, escaped sales opportunities, and untapped potential.

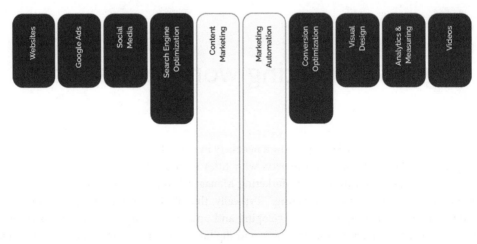

Figure 6.1   The T-model of digital marketing

Agility arises not only from thought patterns but also from processes that sometimes may even feel rigid. Let us take a closer look at a few of the core components on which the agile project management model is based.

A weekly meeting is a weekly 15-minute progress meeting that deals with the marketing conducted for a specific client. The weekly meeting reviews the activities per channel that have already been performed and their impacts, as well as the client's possible new ideas and news. The purpose of the weekly meeting is to keep the entire client team aware of the overall picture of the project and what other team members are doing.

A monthly meeting is a customer-specific monthly meeting that highlights key findings from last month's results and the lessons learned. Typically, a monthly meeting does not cover individual figures in the reports as platform-specific metrics rarely indicate the achievement of business goals or bring in any extra euros to a customer's cash register. The monthly meeting focuses on the future and ensures that the different stages of marketing are mutually support-ive and that the channels in use have the desired balance. At the monthly meeting, marketing planning and implementation are also adapted to the client's business cycles, for example, they are adapted for seasons or product launches.

A retrospective review is a review after the monthly meeting, and it has three main dimen-sions: what has gone well, what has failed, and what could be done better in the next period. By articulating these dimensions and analyzing the customer feedback collected, both the customer team and the whole company consistently achieve better results.

Trello is a project management visualization tool. With Trello, everything you do is made visible to both the client and your colleagues, and no one has to ask about the stage of a single task as it is visible to all with a glance on a Trello card. For example, when a content producer's Trello card that relates to the task of designing downloadable material for use as the spearhead of a social media campaign changes from *review* status to *done* status after the guide has been approved by the client, a social media expert knows that the guide is ready for use in advertising. The purpose of Trello is to make information transparent and thus reduce unnecessary waiting, bottlenecks, and siloed communication.

Slack is an instant messaging application that swept through the ICT world a few years ago and integrates seamlessly with Trello. With Slack, it is possible to communicate with both the team and the client without the messages being lost in an email inbox or other similar channels. Trello also sends notifications to Slack about new cards and the people tagged on them or the comments received. In this way, both the information on the updated Trello cards and the communication between people are available on the same communication channel.

What is it like to do digital marketing in practice? What is a typical week of a digital marketer like and what skills does it require? As a way of answering these questions, in what follows, Lasse, the team coach of Suomen Digimarkkinointi (SDM), talks about his typical working week, which combines agile project management methods with the MRACE® model.

CASE STUDY
CASE EXAMPLE: TYPICAL WORKING WEEK OF A DIGITAL MARKETER

MONDAY: MEETING DAY

I start the work week with a bowl of porridge while preparing for internal meetings. The team's weekly meeting begins at 9 a.m., and before that, I make sure there's enough coffee and that the meeting memo template I prepared the previous week can be found on the Trello board of our team. I decide to add to the agenda a good article that I spotted during the weekend on the challenges and attribute models of measuring multi-channel advertising. I want every team member to at least skim through the article and make notes on the most important findings and new lessons learned to bring to the next week's team meeting. Before the meeting, I still have time to respond to a few Slack messages before it's time to open the Teams connection for the weekly meeting.

The meeting proceeds through a well-honed agenda effortlessly and on schedule, and we will share both customer information and experiences from our newly launched internal quarterly theme. This time the team survives with a fairly small number of tasks, but still, my heart flutters when I see the Trello cards already start popping up during the meeting into the *to do* column on the team wall. I record my own tasks as Trello cards and add a deadline for them, and the team meeting is wrapped up.

I have a couple of hours before the next calendar entry, the team coaches' weekly meeting. Trello's *doing* column starts to get crowded with several small cards, and I'll complete the tasks by reviewing a couple of e-commerce campaigns to ensure that nothing unexpected has occurred during the weekend and that the budgets are adequate for the days to come. The ads I designed for my e-commerce client have produced great results over the weekend, so I'll continue to monitor them later this week.

The content team sends a notification to the client's Slack channel from a blog posted on the website that I will pick up for the Act-stage advertising. The blog will drill down to the client's market and the outlook for the coming year that is aimed at building the client's thought leadership brand positioning. So, I decide to target the ad at both cold and remarketing audiences to spread the firm's expertise also to those who don't yet know this particular brand.

After lunch, I jump into the team coaches' weekly meeting. Team coaches develop the company's processes and solve the challenges that are identified by different teams. We'll go through a couple of questions from the customer base and delve into a messy diagram that some people call a *plan to production process*. From this cause-and-effect jungle, we eventually find some logic, and relying on the process, the diagram that initially seemed challenging is again much clearer and more resistant to human error. Next week's meeting will once again feature a few tasks that will be added as cards that will wait in Trello's *to do* column.

I will dedicate the rest of the afternoon to the client's strategy work. Before that, I quickly respond to countless Slack messages, make the required Trello cards, and silence my notifications because my concentration suffers from continuous distractions.

The strategy work focuses on the current state of the client's digital marketing, the visibility of competitors, the quality of competitors' marketing, and in particular, how these can be used to identify the client's competitive advantages. Putting this strategy into practice involves the design of content for each stage of the MRACE® model and the advertising message appeals to several different buyer personas, which in turn are defined with the client during in-depth buyer persona interviews. The model allows me to define and design engaging and insightful content and advertising that matches all possible stages of the buying process for different buyers. That's how we manage to communicate the right message to the right person at the right time.

TUESDAY: MEETINGS WITH CUSTOMERS AND BRAIN-STORMING

As we have tried to push as many internal and administrative meetings as possible to Mondays, I have three client meetings today. The day starts at 8 a.m. with a client's weekly meeting, where we gather with the client team on the shared Trello wall. We got it quickly started, going through the latest *done* column cards related to different channels. Lots of small tasks have been completed along with the weekly optimization cards, so we can move on to planning for the next couple of weeks' sprints before this client's monthly meeting.

A member of the Google Ads team has noticed that certain new keywords are becoming popular, which immediately gives our copywriter an idea for a blog post theme for the Act stage. We decide to make the implementation of this blog post as a top-priority task so that we can get new, search engine-optimized and sales-oriented content for the client's site. We also build up a fast and straightforward social media funnel in which the readers of the blog will be shown a Convert-stage ad on Facebook and Instagram that aims at lead generation because there is clearly interest in the topic. Fifteen minutes is enough for this, and we will continue the discussion in Slack as the blog topic will immediately spark other thoughts as well. We'll record them on Trello's backlog as there is nothing worse than a forgotten idea.

There will be a short break between meetings. I use it to my advantage by taking a small mind-opening walk. Fifteen minutes of aimless wandering does its job, and I now know how to plan a future recruitment campaign for a client in the ICT industry so that it both supports the employer image and generates high-quality applications. My idea is to hide a few consecutive riddles in the source code of the site, the solutions to which will form the address of a separate landing page. In this way, we can be sure that the candidates who have found their way to the page are both motivated and inventive. I post a campaign idea on the backlog of the client's Trello and tag him on the card. As long as I think the excellent idea resonates with the client as well, the card can be moved from the *to do* column to the *doing* column and production.

After that, the calendar reminds me of a sales meeting that will start in a moment, in which I will participate in the role of an expert in support of the sales rep. We open the Teams connection in advance and make sure that there are no changes to the previous week's Slack discussions and that the customer's needs and goals have remained the same. We're still tweaking the presentation quickly, and soon there will be a beep in the waiting lobby. After the initial chatter and creating favorable atmosphere, we introduce our company to the customer and go through the values on which we base all our work. They seem to resonate particularly well with the client as he admits to emphasizing a value-driven partner in his choices.

We tell him how to reach as large a share of a potential market as possible through channels that interest the client. We find that the customer has not taken content production into account in a recent website overhaul and that it is not very easy to build customized landing pages for campaigns, for example. So, we immediately develop a solution based on search advertising, email automation, and social media that allows us to keep the customer touchpoints on more customizable platforms, and we only use the website for the final conversion where it works. The client also gets excited and promises to get our ideas through to the management team.

The good sales meeting leaves all parties feeling inspired, and I move on to a coffee break with a smile. I quickly scroll through my social media feeds and get back to work.

Before the next weekly meeting of the day, I have time to go through several client projects and make sure the budgets are at the agreed level and advertising is running normally. A few mistakes by artificial intelligence have disapproved products from dynamic ad feeds, so I send a message to Facebook support about these issues. Thoughts about the battle between artificial intelligence and humans come to mind, but I am still not worried about the future.

In the last weekly meeting of the afternoon, I remind the client team about the idea of an e-commerce promotion-code campaign, something that was planned earlier but not yet implemented. Coincidentally, our email campaign expert had also just thought of a similar campaign. So, we decide to combine the power of email and social media to get more subscribers to the Act stage with a newsletter (scheduled for a month later) and to get more audience for social media remarketing campaigns. We'll move the campaign straight to the *doing* phase, and I'll do my share this afternoon. I add the Trello card to the *done* column and the notification to Slack and shut down the computer.

WEDNESDAY: 100 PERCENT PREPARATION, 100 PERCENT PERFORMANCE

By far the biggest focus of the day is on a large-sized client's monthly meeting that will be on Thursday. I want to prepare for the monthly development meeting carefully, so I will open the client's monthly report. At the same time, I open the client's advertising account, website, and Trello wall on another screen to remind me of the big picture.

The figures show what has already been discussed with the client throughout the previous month—the volume of traffic has grown relatively well, but conversions are not following. Conversions are generated, but not in the same proportion to the growth in the volume of traffic. We've launched a couple of different Reach-stage campaigns that are targeted to lookalike audiences, where Facebook uses hundreds of different metrics to find Facebook users who are similar to the current customers and to whom it's worth showing advertising. The quality of traffic generated from these campaigns seems to leave much room for improvement. I plan a few actions to fix the situation and post them on the backlog on their own cards.

On the bright side, a downloadable guide is converting better than in previous months, so there is something positive to say. The advertising for this guide designed for the Act stage has been effective, inexpensive, and comprehensive, so I'll leave it on and reduce the budgets for the Reach stage because traffic alone won't run the client's business. I will invest the saved euros in the Convert-stage campaign, which at least has a large warm audience that has browsed several sub-pages of the website. However, I switch this campaign off for now as I want to hear the client's thoughts in tomorrow's monthly meeting.

I also make sure that the backlog contains the development suggestions I made earlier in addition to this Convert-stage campaign, and I decide to take one suggestion for the Trello wall's *to do* column as it could help scale conversions alongside new campaigns. The other Trello walls have new cards that are expecting new material for the advertisements of several customers. I take care of them during the morning and enjoy the feeling of accomplishment as the cards mostly start to be in the review phase, waiting for client comments.

After lunch, there are two weekly meetings in a row, and they proceed on schedule. The second meeting also includes a client who tells me about a product group whose stock turnover is not satisfactory. We take this group as a target product group in advertising and run a small discount campaign to make room for next season's products. The campaign is run on both Google Ads and social media, but we decide to allocate more budget to the social media because search volumes have started to decline as the season draws to an end. The Trello cards are scheduled to be completed within a week and a half, which is when we agreed to have an interim review of the sales of the product group and decide whether there is still a need to continue the campaign.

After the weekly meeting, I continue my strategy work for a while and build an annual marketing calendar for the client in which big events and trends can be recorded. While certain campaigns should no longer be locked in to certain weeks in the fast-moving and almost chaotic world, it's important to keep in mind the broader understanding of a customer's business environment and customer behavior. For this, the marketing calendar provides a framework in which the predesigned themes, contents, and marketing messages can be flexibly deployed at the right time.

THURSDAY: CONTINUOUS FEEDBACK FACILITATES LEARNING

I take a look at countless emails and Slack messages and take care of the most acute ones before the monthly meeting. A few posts lead to the creation of new Trello cards, most of which are pinned to my wall. Task and time management is made easier when you don't have to memorize everything—the cards remind you of the tasks waiting for you and their due dates.

I jump into the monthly Teams call a few minutes in advance, and we exchange quick thoughts with experts before the client joins the meeting. The team's Growth Owner acts as a facilitator for the meeting and assigning turns to speak, starting with the client, so they can talk about their latest news, business situation, and general mood.

We then review the activities conducted during the previous month, one by one, emphasizing their implications and the lessons we have learned from them. Yesterday's thoughts on the emphasis on the Reach stage are reinforced by speeches from Google Ads and search engine-optimization experts, and when it comes to the time to go through future plans and ideas, I'll introduce the Convert-stage campaign I have planned. We've also noticed that social media results, in particular, show a growing trend in the number of abandoned shopping carts, and we decide to design an email automation that reminds customers to complete a purchase and offers a discount code if the messages alone don't get the desired result. So, we're lifting the Convert-stage campaign from Trello's backlog to the top of the *to do* list as the customer also thinks there should be more conversions. At the same time, a card made by the content team about the email automation appears in the *to do* column, so the idea is almost implemented on the fly.

Other experts are also consulted on bold development proposals regarding the layout of the website, the service promise made there, and the purchase process. Some are immediately taken into implementation, some are left to wait for free resources for the backlog. However, the client's website and digital marketing activities overall are constantly advancing as the backlog feeds in new ideas and ensures that there is fuel for development.

Despite its efficiency, the hour-long meeting is slightly extended. However, we still ask the customer for feedback on our operations and the smoothness of our cooperation because if the feedback cycle remains frequent, possible negative feelings are not enlarged into bigger problems. The customer is also prepared to give feedback, this time mostly positive. It feels good and encourages us to keep up the good work—although there is always room for constructive criticism that facilitates learning and development.

After the meeting, we will have a retrospective meeting regarding the previous month in which we will stop to look back on the period and try to see where we succeeded and, above all, what we could develop in the future. This time we are focusing on the team's views. We unanimously state that the client's goals have remained well at the center of our efforts and we have taken the right steps but could put even more effort into developing multi-channel campaigns. The client also provides a large amount of individual advertising material, the processing of which in social media could well be automated, which would free up resources for optimizing and developing advertising from the manual construction of advertisements. I'll make this a card for myself in Trello's backlog so I can go through it with the client later.

The rest of the day is based on sales support and customer work. The sales team have come to Slack with good questions about a few interesting customers, and I'm pleased to notice that other experts on my team have filled the Slack chain with their posts. Experiences and observations from different industries are rapidly appearing in the message chain and my responsibility is limited to formulating appropriate service packages and budget recommendations.

I'm still doing a regular review for my clients and making sure the campaigns are alright, budgets remain at the agreed levels, and that the results are coming in. There are no surprises, so the day can be wrapped up.

FRIDAY: A FLOW STATE

Friday is a meeting-free day, when you can usually delve into larger entities for as long as you want without external interruptions. We found out earlier that short interruptions are the worst time thieves and that it took a tremendous amount of time and mental resources to move from one task to another or to reassemble an interrupted idea. So, we liberated Fridays from meetings, which has worked.

The morning goes by normally, responding to messages, but after ten I turn off Slack and email and switch the phone to silent mode. This allows me to focus on strategy work without interruption. Buyer personas are starting to take shape one by one. Deepening the client's business and its development is so immersive that I must force myself to interrupt my work for lunch.

In the afternoon, I have set aside time to develop the campaign structures for two different clients. The MRACE® model works optimally when you can provide interesting, insightful, and relevant content to the buyer at every stage. For both of these clients, it is beginning to feel that the contents of the different stages are not fully balanced. So, I map out the content pieces in use and the social media campaigns that drive traffic to them, as well as their budget weightings. However, I notice that no exact content has been created for the Convert stage in either client case for a while.

Through Slack, we devised a few article topics and process descriptions with the content team to help a customer who is on the verge of making a purchase figure out responses to the last counter-arguments and barriers to making a purchase on the website. I post the topics at the title level as Trello cards in the client's backlogs, and in the second case, the customer himself gets so excited that he promises to write the raw version himself during the weekend.

The working week is coming to an end. I'm still taking a look at the deadlines of my own Trello wall *doing* cards and make sure I've had time to do all the most urgent tasks this week. Next week's meetings don't require special preparation this time, so I'll shut down my computer and work-related communication channels and leave for the weekend!

7
In closing: the future of digital marketing

Not even half of today's digital marketing could have been made five years ago. Tools and marketing technologies are evolving at such a tremendous rate that it is hard to imagine what kind of situation we will be in five years from now.

It is said that the golden age of marketing technology began in the early 2010s. At that time, forms of marketing that are taken for granted today—such as marketing automation, chatbots, Google advertising, and social media advertising—began to become more common. Since then, various SaaS-type marketing tools have been released on a practically daily basis, which is mostly a good thing but also a bad thing. Namely, we humans love different tools, which in the context of marketing easily leads companies to buy great-sounding tools and technologies without even thinking about whether they will solve the real problems the company has in its marketing. The plethora of tools and technologies easily overwhelm you, making the overall picture of marketing forgotten.

But why was the golden age of marketing technology in the early 2010s when technologies are being developed every day more and faster than before? It is true that the tools have evolved a lot in ten years, but no new and groundbreaking tool has emerged in recent years. It has been said, therefore, that we are currently living in the backwaters of digital marketing and marketing technology. However, we firmly believe that today's trends—such as AI, 5G, blockchains, and digital ecosystems—will revolutionize digital marketing in a few years, just as today's self-evident tools did in the early 2010s.

Indeed, the second golden age of marketing technology is expected to begin by 2025 (Figure 7.1). Companies that do not develop, manage, and measure their marketing based on a particular model will not be able to adopt new technologies with the efficiency required by change. The second golden age of digital marketing and marketing technology will change digital marketing more than we can imagine. The best way to prepare for it is to put in place a marketing model that will withstand change. You have just learned one of these models from this book.

Now that you have read the entire book, you should have a better idea of how to create a digital marketing strategy for your organization, how to implement it, and how to measure its results. Remember that not everything can and should be learned at once. If you feel like there was a lot in this book, keep in mind that good marketing only requires the following three things: the customer's identified need, the product, and the story of how the product solves the customer's need. Everything is built around this frame. So, keep going on your learning path because knowing the things in this book on a practical level will open countless new doors in your life.

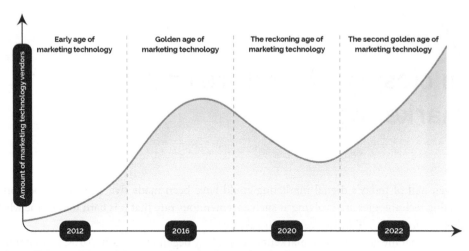

Figure 7.1   The golden age of marketing technologies

Marketing is a skill that requires a deep understanding of, among other things, business, the competitive field, trends, buying behavior, technologies, and human psychology. Marketing is no longer a support function on the periphery of the business but one of the pulsating cores at the heart of the business. Marketing has gained its rightful place. Now it is your turn to take your rightful place as a marketing professional.

BIBLIOGRAPHY

BOOKS

Chaffey, D. & Ellis-Chadwick, F. (2019). *Digital marketing* (7th edn). Harlow: Pearson.

Chaffey, D. & Smith, P.R. (2017). *Digital marketing excellence: Planning, optimizing and integrating online marketing* (5th edn). London: Routledge.

De Pelsmacker, P., Geuens, M., & Van Den Bergh, J. (2021). *Marketing communications eBook ePub: A European perspective* (7th edn). Harlow: Pearson.

Godin, S. (2018). *This is marketing: You can't be seen until you learn to see.* London: Penguin Books.

HubSpot (2017). Content trends: Preferences emerge along generational fault lines (author Mimi An), November 6, available at: https://blog.hubspot.com/marketing/content-trends-preferences (accessed March 1, 2023).

Hu, H.-F. & Krishen, A.S. (2019). Information overload in the digital age. In A.S. Krishen & O. Berezan (eds), *Marketing and humanity: Discourses in the real world* (pp. 185–203). Newcastle upon Tyne: Cambridge Scholars Publishing.

Jackson, S. (2015). *Cult of analytics: Data analytics for marketing* (2nd edn). London: Routledge.

Karjaluoto, H. (2010). *Digitaalinen markkinointiviestintä—Esimerkkejä parhaista käytännöistä yritys- ja kuluttajamarkkinointiin.* Jyväskylä: Docendo.

Karjaluoto, H. (2021). How consumer attitudes and values change (In Finnish: Miten kuluttajien asenteet ja arvot muuttuvat?), Foundation of Retail Research & Finnish Commerce Federation (In Finnish: Vähittäiskaupan tutkimussäätiö & Kaupan Liitto), survey study, available at: https://vkts.fi (accessed March 1, 2023).

Kotler, P. & Keller, K.L. (2021). *Marketing management* (15th edn). Harlow: Pearson.

Kotler, P., Kartajaya, H., & Setiawan, I. (2017). *Marketing 4.0: Moving from traditional to digital.* Hoboken, NJ: Wiley.

Mero, J., Karjaluoto, H., & Tammisalo, T. (2021). How a glass processing SME developed its Big Data competence. In Carsten Lund Pedersen, Adam Lindgreen, Thomas Ritter, & Torsten Ringberg (eds), *Big Data in small business: Data-driven growth in small and medium-sized enterprises* (pp. 117–27). Cheltenham, UK and Northampton, MA, USA: Edward Elgar Publishing.

Opresnik, M.O., Kotler, P., & Hollensen, S. (2021). *Social media marketing: A practitioner guide* (4th edn). Lübeck: Opresnik Management Guides.

Peppers, D., Rogers, M., & Kotler, P. (2017). *Managing customer relationships.* Hoboken, NJ: Wiley.

Porter, M.E. (2008). *Competitive strategy: Techniques for analyzing industries and competitors.* New York: Free Press.

Sawhney, M. (2011). Lowe's Companies Inc.: Optimizing the marketing communications mix. Kellog School of Management.

Solomon, M.R., Hogg, M.K., Askegaard, S., & Bamossy, G. (2019). *Consumer behaviour. A European perspective.* Harlow: Pearson.

SCIENTIFIC ARTICLES

Aslam, B. & Karjaluoto, H. (2017). Digital advertising around paid spaces, e-advertising industry's revenue engine: A review and research agenda. *Telematics and Informatics*, 34 (8), 1650–62.

Avery, J., Fournier, S., & Wittenbraker, J. (2014). Unlock the mysteries of your customer relationships. Are you connecting with consumers the way they want you to? *Harvard Business Review*, 92 (7/8), 72–81.

Carrozzi, A., Chylinski, M., Heller, J., Hilken, T., Keeling, D.I., & de Ruyter, K. (2019). What's mine is a hologram? How shared augmented reality augments psychological ownership. *Journal of Interactive Marketing*, 48, 71–88.

De Haan, E., Kannan, P.K., Verhoef, P.C., & Wiesel, T. (2018). Device switching in online purchasing: Examining the strategic contingencies. *Journal of Marketing*, 82, 1–19.

Djafarova, E. & Rushworth, C. (2017). Exploring the credibility of online celebrtities' Instagram profiles in influencing the purchase decisions of young female users. *Computers in Human Behavior*, 68, 1–7.

Doran, G.T. (1981). There's a S.M.A.R.T. way to write management's goals and objectives. *Management Review*, 70 (11), 35–6.

Dwivedi, Y.K., Hughes, L., Ismagilova, E. et al. (2021a). Artificial Intelligence (AI): Multidisciplinary perspectives on emerging challenges, opportunities, and agenda for research, practice and policy. *International Journal of Information Management*, 57, 101994.

Dwivedi, Y.K., Ismagilova, E., Hughes, D.L. et al (2021b). Setting the future of digital and social media marketing research: Perspectives and research propositions. *International Journal of Information Management*, 59, 102168.

Edelman, D.C. & Singer, M. (2015). Competing on customer journeys. *Harvard Business Review*, 93 (11), 88–94.

Foltean, F.S., Trif, S.M., & Tuleu, D.L. (2019). Customer relationship management capabilities and social media technology use: Consequences on firm performance. *Journal of Business Research*, 104, 563–75.

Fulgoni, G.M. & Lipsman, A. (2017). The downside of digital word of mouth and the pursuit of media quality. *Journal of Advertising Research*, 57 (2), 127–31.

Gu, X. & Kannan, P.K. (2021). The dark side of mobile app adoption: Examining the impact on customers' multichannel purchase. *Journal of Marketing Research*, 58 (2), 246–64.

Gu, X., Kannan, P.K., & Ma, L. (2018). Selling the premium in freemium. *Journal of Marketing*, 82 (6), 10–27.

Gupta, S., Leszkiewicz, A., Kumar, V., Bijmolt, T., & Potapov, D. (2020). Digital analytics: Modeling for insights and new methods. *Journal of Interactive Marketing*, 51, 26–43.

Haenlain, M. (2017). How to date your clients in the 21st century: Challenges in managing customer relationships in today's world. *Business Horizons*, 60 (5), 577–86.

Hepola, J., Karjaluoto, H., & Hintikka, A. (2017). The effect of sensory brand experience and involvement on brand equity directly and indirectly through consumer brand engagement. *Journal of Product & Brand Management*, 26 (3), 282–93.

Hollebeek, L.D. & Macky, K. (2019). Digital content marketing's role in fostering consumer engagement, trust, and value: Framework, fundamental propositions, and implications. *Journal of Interactive Marketing*, 45, 27–41.

Huang, M.-H. & Rust, R.T. (2021). A strategic framework for artificial intelligence in marketing. *Journal of the Academy of Marketing Science*, 49, 30–50.

Iacobucci, D., Petrescu, M., Krishen, A., & Bendixen, M. (2019). The state of marketing analytics in research and practice. *Journal of Marketing Analytics*, 7 (3), 152–81.

Järvinen, J. & Karjaluoto, H. (2015). The use of Web analytics for digital marketing performance measurement. *Industrial Marketing Management*, 50, 117–27.

Järvinen, J. & Taiminen, H. (2016). Harnessing marketing automation for B2B content marketing. *Industrial Marketing Management*, 54, 164–75.

Kannan, P.K. & Li, H.A. (2017). Digital marketing: A framework, review and research agenda. *International Journal of Research in Marketing*, 34, 22–45.

Karjaluoto, H,. Hänninen, N., & Ulkuniemi, P. (2015). The role of digital channels in industrial marketing communications. *Journal of Business & Industrial Marketing*, 30 (6), 703–10.

Labrecque, L I., vor dem Esche, J., Mathwick, C., Novak, T.P., & Hofacker, C F. (2013). Consumer power: Evolution in the digital age. *Journal of Interactive Marketing*, 27(4), 257–69.

Lafley, A.G. & Martin, R. (2017). Customer loyalty is overrated. *Harvard Business Review*, 95 (1), 47–54.

Lamberton, C. & Stephen, A.T. (2016). A thematic exploration of digital, social media, and mobile marketing research evolution from 2000 to 2015 and an agenda for future inquiry. *Journal of Marketing*, 80 (6), 146–72.

Lee, D., Hosanagar, K., & Nair, H.S. (2018). Advertising content and consumer engagement on social media: Evidence from Facebook. *Management Science*, 64 (11), 5105–31.

Lee, J., Park, D.H., & Han, I. (2008). The effect of negative online consumer reviews on product attitude: An information processing view. *Electronic Commerce Research and Applications*, 7 (3), 341–52.

Lemon, K. & Verhoef, P. (2016). Understanding customer experience throughout the customer journey. *Journal of Marketing*, 80 (6), 69–96.

Li, F., Larimo, J., & Leonidou, L.C. (2021). Social media marketing strategy: Definition, conceptualization, taxonomy, validation, and future agenda. *Journal of the Academy of Marketing Science*, 49, 51–70.

Lipiäinen, H. & Karjaluoto, H. (2015a). The usage of digital marketing channels in SMEs. *Journal of Small Business and Enterprise Development*, 22 (4), 633–51.

Lipiäinen, H. & Karjaluoto, H. (2015b). Industrial branding in the digital age. *Journal of Business & Industrial Marketing*, 30 (6), 733–41.

Liu, Q.B. & Karahanna, E. (2017). The dark side of reviews: The swaying effects of online product reviews on attribute preference construction. *MIS Quarterly*, 41 (2), 427–48.

Mero, J., Tarkiainen, A., & Tobon, J. (2020). Effectual and causal reasoning in the adoption of marketing automation. *Industrial Marketing Management*, 86, 212–22.

Munnukka, J., Karjaluoto, H., & Tikkanen, A. (2015). Are Facebook community members really loyal to the brand? *Computers in Human Behavior*, 51, 429–39.

Namin, A., Hamilton, M.L., & Rohm, A.J. (2017). Impact of message design on banner advertising involvement and effectiveness: An empirical investigation. *Journal of Marketing Communications*, 26 (2), 115–29.

Porter, M.E. (1979). How competitive forces shape strategy. *Harvard Business Review*, 57 (2), 137–45.

Rai, A. (2020). Explainable AI: From black box to glass box. *Journal of the Academy of Marketing Science*, 48 (1), 137–41.

Ritz, W., Wolf, M., & McQuitty, S. (2019). Digital marketing adoption and success for small businesses. *Journal of Research in Interactive Marketing*, 13 (2), 179–203.

Saarijärvi, H., Karjaluoto, H., & Kuusela, H. (2013). Extending customer relationship management: From empowering firms to empowering customers. *Journal of Systems & Information Technology*, 15 (2), 140–58.

Salonen, V. & Karjaluoto, H. (2016). Web personalization: The state of the art and future avenues for research and practice. *Telematics and Informatics*, 33 (4), 1088–104.

Salonen, V. & Karjaluoto, H. (2019). About time: A motivation-based complementary framework for temporal dynamics in web personalization. *Journal of Systems and Information Technology*, 21 (2), 236–54.

Salonen, V., Munnukka, J., & Karjaluoto, H. (2020). The role of fundamental motivations in willingness-to-pay online. *Journal of Retailing and Consumer Services*, 52, 101930.

Sanakulov, N., Kalliomaa, S., & Karjaluoto, H. (2018). Salesperson adoption and usage of mobile sales configuration tools. *Journal of Systems and Information Technology*, 20 (2), 168–90.

Shaikh, A.A. & Karjaluoto, H. (2015). Making the most of information technology & systems usage: A literature review, framework and future research agenda. *Computers in Human Behavior*, 49, 541–66.

Shareef, M.A., Mukerji, B., Alryalat, M.A.A., Wright, A., & Dwivedi, Y.K. (2018). Advertisements on Facebook: Identifying the persuasive elements in the development of positive attitudes in consumers. *Journal of Retailing and Consumer Services*, 43, 258–68.

Shareef, M.A., Mukerji, B., Dwivedi, Y.K., Rana, N.P., & Islam, R. (2019). Social media marketing: Comparative effect of advertisement sources. *Journal of Retailing and Consumer Services*, 46, 58–69.

Shiau, W.L., Dwivedi, Y.K., & Yang, H.S. (2017). Co-citation and cluster analyses of extant literature on social networks. *International Journal of Information Management*, 37 (5), 390–99.

Simons, R. (2014). Choosing the right customer. The first step in a winning strategy. *Harvard Business Review*, 92 (3), 48–55.

Singh, J.P., Irani, S., Rana, N.P., Dwivedi, Y.K., Saumya, S., & Roy, P.K. (2017). Predicting the "helpfulness" of online consumer reviews. *Journal of Business Research*, 70, 346–55.

Sivarajah, U., Irani, Z., Gupta, S., & Mahroof, K. (2020). Role of big data and social media analytics for business to business sustainability: A participatory web context. *Industrial Marketing Management*, 86, 163–79.

Sousa, M.J. & Rocha, Á. (2019). Skills for disruptive digital business. *Journal of Business Research*, 94, 257–63.

Sun, S., Hall, D.J., & Cegielski, C.G. (2019). Organizational intention to adopt big data in the B2B context: An integrated view. *Industrial Marketing Management*, 86, 109–21.

Syrdal, H.A. & Briggs, E. (2018). Engagement with social media content: A qualitative exploration. *The Journal of Marketing Theory and Practice*, 26 (1–2), 4–22.

Taiminen, K. & Karjaluoto, H. (2017). Examining the performance of brand-extended thematic-content: The divergent impact of avid- and skim-reader groups. *Computers in Human Behavior*, 72, 449–58.
Toman, N., Adamson, B., & Gomez, C. (2017). The new sales imperative. *Harvard Business Review*, 95, 118–25.
Tyrväinen, O. & Karjaluoto, H. (2019a). A systematic literature review and analysis of mobile retailing adoption. *Journal of Internet Commerce*, 18 (2), 221–47.
Tyrväinen, O. & Karjaluoto, H. (2019b). Omnichannel experience—towards successful channel integration in retail. *Journal of Customer Behaviour*, 18 (1), 17–34.
Tyrväinen, O., Karjaluoto, H., & Saarijärvi, H. (2020). Personalization and hedonic motivation in creating customer experiences and loyalty in omnichannel retail. *Journal of Retailing and Consumer Services*, 57, 102233.
Wang, Z. & Kim, H.G. (2017). Can social media marketing improve customer relationship capabilities and firm performance? Dynamic capability perspective. *Journal of Interactive Marketing*, 39, 15–26.
Zolfagharian, M. & Yazdanparast, A. (2017). The dark side of consumer life in the age of virtual and mobile technology. *Journal of Marketing Management*, 33 (15–16), 1304–35.

INTERNET SOURCES

Alltherooms (2021). April 21, available at: https://www.alltherooms.com/analytics/airbnb-statistics (accessed March 1, 2023).
Boostlikes (2013; updated 2022). 10 Celebrities that have bought Twitter followers, available at: https://boostlikes.com/blog/2013/10/10-celebrities-bought-twitter-followers (accessed March 1, 2023).
Braineet (2021). My Starbucks idea: An open innovation case-study, available at: https://www.braineet.com/blog/my-starbucks-idea-case-study (accessed March 1, 2023).
Chaffey, D. (2021). Introducing The RACE Framework: a practical framework to improve your digital marketing, May 27, available at: https://www.smartinsights.com/digital-marketing-strategy/race-a-practical-framework-to-improve-your-digital-marketing/ (accessed March 1, 2023).
Chiefmartec (n.d.), blog text, available at: https://chiefmartec.com (accessed March 1, 2023).
Dwoskin, E. & Timberg, C. (2018). How merchants use Facebook to flood Amazon with fake reviews, *Washington Post*, April 23, available at: https://www.washingtonpost.com/business/economy/how-merchants-secretly-use-facebook-to-flood-amazon-with-fake-reviews/2018/04/23/5dad1e30-4392-11e8-8569-26fda6b404c7_story.html (accessed March 1, 2023).
Forbes (2019). The 80% blind spot: Are you ignoring unstructured organizational data? (author Adam Rogers), January 29, available at: https://www.forbes.com/sites/forbestechcouncil/2019/01/29/the-80-blind-spot-are-you-ignoring-unstructured-organizational-data/ (accessed March 1, 2023).
GE Capital Retail Bank (2013). Second Annual Major Purchase Shopper Study, July 12, available at: https://www.ge.com/news/press-releases/ge-capital-retail-banks-second-annual-shopper-study-outlines-digital-path-major (accessed March 1, 2023).
Google & ComScore (2017). Automotive Shopper Study (N = 3,165 consumers 18+, who had purchased a car duing the last three months), January, available at: https://www.thinkwithgoogle.com/consumer-insights/consumer-trends/digital-car-research-statistics/ (accessed March 1, 2023).
HubSpot (2017). Content trends: Preferences emerge along generational fault lines (author Mimi An), November 6, available at: https://blog.hubspot.com/marketing/content-trends-preferences
MRACE-malli (2021). https://www.digimarkkinointi.fi/mrace-malli (accessed March 1, 2023).
Salsify (2017). Second Annual Cracking the Consumer Code (N = 1,000), available at: https://www.salsify.com/content/ebook-2017-consumer-research-report-cracking-the-code (accessed March 1, 2023).
Uberflip (2021). The Experience Disconnect: B2B Marketing Report, available at: https://www.uberflip.com/the-experience-disconnect-2021-b2b-marketing-report/ (accessed March 1, 2023).
UM (2019). Wave X Remix Culture Study, available at: https://wavex.umww.com
Unilever (2021). Innovate with us, available at: https://www.unilever.com/brands/innovation/open-innovation/ (accessed March 1, 2023).
Wikipedia (2021). SMART criteria, available at: https://en.wikipedia.org/wiki/SMART_criteria (accessed March 1, 2023).

ZME Science (2021). Your smartphone is millions of times more powerful than the Apollo 11 guidance computers, May 13, available at: https://www.zmescience.com/science/news-science/smartphone-power-compared-to-apollo-432/ (accessed March 1, 2023).

INDEX